# ANGELS *in the* REALMS *of* HEAVEN

DESTINY IMAGE BOOKS BY KEVIN BASCONI

*Dancing with Angels 1—How To Work With The Angels In Your Life*

*Dancing with Angels 2—The Role of the Holy Spirit and Open Heavens in Activating Angelic Encounters in Your Life*

# ANGELS *in the* REALMS *of* HEAVEN

## THE REALITY OF ANGELIC MINISTRY TODAY

# KEVIN BASCONI

DESTINY IMAGE® PUBLISHERS, INC.
P.O. Box 310, Shippensburg, PA 17257-0310
*"Promoting Inspired Lives."*

This book and all other Destiny Image, Revival Press, MercyPlace, Fresh Bread, Destiny Image Fiction, and Treasure House books are available at Christian bookstores and distributors worldwide.

For a U.S. bookstore nearest you, call 1-800-722-6774.
For more information on foreign distributors, call 717-532-3040.
Reach us on the Internet: www.destinyimage.com.

ISBN 13 TP: 978-0-7684-0291-9
ISBN 13 Ebook: 978-0-7684-8798-5

For Worldwide Distribution, Printed in the U.S.A.
3 4 5 6 7 8 / 16 15 14 13 12

This
book
is
dedicated
to
God the Father, God the Son, and God the Holy Spirit.
without
You
Guys
none
of
this
would
have
been
possible!

# Acknowledgment

I want to thank my wonderful wife, Kathy, for her enduring love, kindness, patience, long hours of proofreading, and help with the entire process of writing these books.

I love you!

I want to personally thank the editors who worked on this book - whoever you are!

Fine Job!

# Endorsements

When Kevin Basconi had his encounters with angels and visited the heavenly realms, it transformed his life and drew him into the secret place of intimacy. I believe as you read these amazing third heaven experiences, the anointing for deeper intimacy with God will rub off on you.

Sid Roth
Host, *It's Supernatural!*

Kevin is the real deal. He has almost daily encounters with heaven and the angelic and sees unusual miracles as a result on the earth. Kevin will take you on a journey that will open your eyes to the realm of heaven like you have never known before. "On earth as it is in heaven" will take on a whole new literal meaning as you read this book. You will also discover an entire host of angels waiting to minister with you and accelerate everything you are called to do as your intimacy with God explodes into new levels you never knew existed.

David Herzog
Author of Glory Invasion
Co-host of "The Glory Zone" TV show
www.thegloryzone.org

I don't know anyone better positioned to challenge you to rise above powerless living and embrace the reality of heaven than Kevin Basconi. For too long Christians have embraced a miniscule vision of what our heavenly home will look like, and what angels are doing in heaven today is satisfied with merely marveling at the supernatural experiences we see in the Bible.

Kevin casts a bold vision for what the reality of heaven was always designed to look like. Kevin's combination of revelation, raw passion, and practicality will move you to want to live at a higher level of the supernatural and equip you to get there. This book is enthralling and moves you to believe in the impossible as you learn more fully the reality of heaven. *Angels in the Realm of Heaven* has my highest recommendation!

BRIAN LAKE
Founder, Brian Lake Ministries
Senior Pastor, Keepers of the Flame International Church
Author, Romancing the King

Kevin Basconi's trilogy is full of insight, revelation, and records of fascinating encounters he has had with angels and the supernatural realm of the Kingdom of God. In his third book in the Dancing with Angels series, *Angels in the Realms of Heaven,* he vividly shares the duties and activities of God's angels in their specific assignments in Heaven. You will read detailed accounts of Kevin's heavenly experiences in the past ten years in addition to descriptions of various terrains in the Father's domain. The reality of Heaven will be awakened in you as you read this book.

PATRICIA KING
Founder, XPministries
XPmedia.com

Kevin has done it again! *Angels in the Realms of Heaven* will inspire, intrigue, and amaze you. Most importantly, reading this book will demonstrate the practical side of hearing and seeing what God is doing in your life. Kevin gives firsthand examples of how encounters he has had gave insight and direction for the actions he needed to take. The bottom line: hearing from God is very practical! You will walk away from reading this book with a renewed passion for knowing what your Father is doing as well as tangible insights into how you can experience the realms of Heaven. Thank you—and way to go, Kevin!

ALAN KOCH
Senior Pastor Christ Triumphant Church
Lee's Summit, Missouri

Kevin Basconi is one of those rare gems in the Kingdom of God who affords the Body of Christ, and the world, the wonderful opportunity to see beyond the veil into the heavenly realms. His personal experiences with the Lord and with Heaven and angels will energize your faith. His writings, without a doubt, will awaken your imagination to a whole new world of eternal hope.

MICHAEL A. DANFORTH
Mountain Top International
Yakima, Washington

In *Angels in the Realm of Heaven,* Kevin takes you on incredible journeys into Heaven! His thrilling testimonies will fascinate you and create great hunger for more intimacy with God. Just as his dramatic heavenly encounters with angels radically changed his life, you too can have life-transforming angelic encounters as you read this awe-inspiring book.

GARY OATES
Author, *Open My Eyes, Lord*
International Conference Speaker

In *Angels in the Realm of Heaven,* Kevin Basconi, through his own personal encounters, gives us some inspirational and encouraging glimpses into the inheritance reserved and awaiting every believer in Jesus. Although Kevin does a wonderful job in explaining what he saw and experienced, it is obvious no words can even begin to fully describe what Heaven is like. Reading this book leaves the reader with an almost unexplainable longing and hope for what eternity holds. It also will ignite within you a hunger to experience what the Lord meant when He said in Ephesians how He has "raised us up together, and made us sit together in the heavenly places in Christ Jesus."

DAVID WHITE<br>
Pastor MorningStar Fellowship Church<br>
Moravian Falls, North Carolina

In John 1.51, Jesus makes this declaration: "Most assuredly, I say to you, hereafter you shall see heaven open and the angels of God ascending and descending upon the Son of Man." We live in an hour where the reality of this statement is being fulfilled, and the realms of heaven and angelic ministry according to Hebrews 1.7,14 are opening and escalating. Kevin is a man who over the past decade has had many experiences which confirm this dynamic of the Kingdom Of Heaven. In this book, Angels In the Realms of Heaven, Kevin shares his journey, recounting personal testimonies, and establishing a solid Scriptural foundation for these kinds of life changing encounters with Christ and His Kingdom, and encourages the reader to access the realms of Heaven and embark on their own journeys with Jesus.

Pastor Scott Nelson<br>
New City Church<br>
Kalamazoo, Michigan

It's fascinating to take part of Kevin's experiences of interacting with angels. These revelations bring forth insight and knowledge of spiritual keys from the Master's hand, and they are very precious. And then the Spirit of truth will guide you in line with the Word to the glory to God.

Those who are workers for Christ should yearn to be like in Isaiah 49:2 "In his quiver he hid me", to attain his eternal purpose. To be hidden long in secret places where all supernatural experience have been birthed, where the ordinary church people can awaken their spiritual senses hungering and thirsting for the reality of the heavenly realms, where the Lord says: "I will give you the treasures of darkness and hidden riches of secret places" Isa. 45:3. We have the privilege of knowing Kevin and Kathy for several years. They have been a great inspiration for us, and during the last year the Lord in His grace has increased the frequency of open heavens, angelic visitations, and visions in our lives. We hope that this book will give you a hunger for more of the Lord and His Heaven along with an understanding of the heavenly realities.

PASTOR PER and MAJBRITT ALTSVED
Christ's Church, Stockholm Sweden

*Let not your heart be troubled; you believe in God, believe also in Me. In My Father's house are many mansions; if it were not so, I would have told you. I go to prepare a place for you. And if I go and prepare a place for you, I will come again and receive you to Myself; that where I am, there you may be also. And where I go you know, and the way you know* (John 14:1-4).

# CONTENTS

# PROLOGUE

Please allow me to start by stating emphatically: "It's all about You, Jesus."

In the first two books of this trilogy, the majority of the angelic visitations or encounters that are depicted occurred upon the earth or in the "terrestrial realm." In this third book, I share a number of dramatic "heavenly" angelic encounters. These kinds of heavenly, angelic testimonies are referred to throughout both of the preceding books in this trilogy. The stage for the third book of this trilogy was set by one of the final two chapters of the second book entitled *Anointed to Reign as Priests and Prophets and Understanding Your Role as a Royal Priest After the Order of Melchizedek.*

In those concluding chapters of the second book, I describe powerful "third heaven" or "heavenly" angelic visitations or angelic encounters that transpired in the "courtroom of Heaven." I encouraged you that these types of experiences were modeled for us by Jesus Christ, and they are freely available to us today. Those testimonies preview, or foreshadow more testimonies of this heavenly or supernatural nature. They were designed to lay a foundation, prepare your heart, and open the door for the powerful contents of this third book.

Jesus Himself referred to these kinds of supernatural experiences and heavenly places in John 14:1-6:

> *Let not your heart be troubled; you believe in God, believe also in Me. In My Father's house are many mansions; if it were not so, I would have told you. I go to prepare a place for you. And if I go and prepare a place for you, I will come again and receive you to Myself; that where I am, there you may be also. And where I go you know, and the way you know. Thomas said to Him, "Lord, we do not know where You are going, and how can we know the way?" Jesus said to him, "I am the way, the truth, and the life. No one comes to the Father except through Me."*

In my previous two books in the Dancing With Angels series, *How to Work with the Angels in Your Life* and *The Role of the Holy Spirit and Open Heavens in Activating Angelic Encounters in Your Life*, I have enumerated upon many angelic visitations and outlined scriptural principles that can open the realm of angelic activity to ordinary folks. Again, most of the angelic visitations and encounters documented in the first two books of this trilogy were illustrations of angelic visitations that occurred upon the earth or in the temporal realm. In this book, I share with you many other angelic encounters that occurred in the spiritual or heavenly realm. I do not wish to enter into the semantics of the location concerning these angelic encounters. However, I can safely say that they all transpired in the "heavenly realms."

It is not really important if these encounters transpired in the third heaven, the seventh heaven, or in which part or realm of Heaven. What is important is that these encounters with Christ and His angels took place in heavenly places. As a result, I can relate to you detailed portraits and descriptions of the places that I walked through in Heaven, or the heavenly realms. These angelic experiences occurred in the spiritual realm, but that does not invalidate their importance or impact upon my life. Hopefully these testimonies will encourage and inspire you as you read them. In fact, several people who have read excerpts from this book were moved to tears of hope and joy. Heaven is a real place; and this book describes Heaven's appearance and heavenly activity with clarity and great detail.

This book was actually birthed back in 2001. As a new believer, the Lord instructed me to write and record the supernatural encounters that I was experiencing. I chronicled most of the heavenly experiences and angelic visitations recorded in this book in 2001 and 2002. However, I also have included other significant heavenly angelic encounters from more recent dates. Most of the early angelic experiences were documented immediately after I would "return" to my little house at 121 Beech Street from the realm of the heavens. Those original documents have been transcribed, edited, and written in this book in their original context with minor grammatical corrections and occasional addendums for clarity.

## FRESH AND PRISTINE

The point is that these angelic and heavenly visitations have a fresh and pristine character. These testimonies and accounts of Heaven are unadulterated by indoctrination into any system of dogmatic religious doctrinal belief structure. They are based squarely on the content of the canon of Scripture and searching my old King James Bible. They are based upon my encounters with the Messiah, Jesus Christ of Nazareth. He is not dead, He is alive, and He still visits folks today to minister to them one on one. Jesus still leaves the ninety-nine to go after the one lost sheep. He still loves each of us with a supernatural love that is impossible for us to comprehend with our human intellect. In other words, the experiences documented in this book are the innocent renderings of events as written down by a "babe in Christ." At the time many of these heavenly experiences were recorded, I was not well-read, nor had I studied the Bible to any great degree. In my opinion, this fact lends validity to these simple, supernatural and ethereal observations of a new believer.

As I was preparing this manuscript, I was in the process of transcribing these digitally recorded documents into a usable format to submit to the publisher. During this time I prayed about the Lord's purpose for this book. I hope that these simple testimonies of my experiences in Heaven will in some way inspire and build in you a sense of your heavenly home. I will share these experiences as unpretentiously as possible, and I have sought to include the dates that each episode transpired where possible.

In the passage of Scripture quoted from John 14, Jesus speaks of "My Father's house" and "many mansions." Jesus also told us that He was the "way" to the Father's mansions. Since these events began to transpire over a decade ago, I have had a lot of time to pray and seek the Lord about them. I have meditated upon what I experienced, and I have pondered them in my heart repeatedly for more than ten years. Assuredly I say to you that I was reluctant to share them at all. I consider these heavenly experiences holy and special kisses from the Messiah.

I have asked the Lord what I was really experiencing and where exactly I was taken to in these heavenly experiences. It is possible that the large stone castle or home that I visited in the heavens was actually my heavenly mansion or home. However, it is also possible that I also visited the Father's actual house on numerous occasions (see John 14:2). I believe that I was actually in Heaven during these experiences. I will describe these places in great detail and hopefully give you glimpses into the realms of Heaven. Along this journey we will also see how angels move about, appear, and seem to "work" in the heavenly realms. May we all greet one another in that place one day. Heaven is real! And Christ has already prepared a place for you to dwell with Him in Paradise. Your heavenly home awaits you.

## FATHER'S HOUSE

The words "Father's house" found in John 14 can be literally translated as *oikia,* meaning: properly a residence or home (abstractly), but usually (concretely) an abode (literally or figuratively); referring to an actual structure or building, and by implication the property of a single family (especially domestics): -home, house (-hold).

It is possible that Jesus is referring to our heavenly inheritance as an engrafted child of God. We are a valuable part of God's extended family. We are sons and daughters of God. You are a joint heir with Christ who has a supernatural inheritance laid up for you in the heavenly realms. Personally, I find this quite exciting, and I hope that this book will spark your interest and passion to press into the Kingdom of God and receive your heavenly inheritance. By the way, you need not die to visit Heaven.

However, the Bible clearly teaches and illustrates that we have a real home to look forward to in Heaven when we die and depart from this earth or temporal realm. Our spirits will live on for eternity with Christ in the realms of Heaven—provided that we believe that Jesus Christ is our Messiah, or Savior, and we choose to accept God's offer of free salvation. Entering Heaven is conditional, and we must choose it. Jesus uses the Greek word *menó*. John 14 is saying that there are "many mansions" in His Father's house, or in Heaven; the Greek word *menó* is similar to *oikia*. Again, meaning a place to stay, a residence, an abode or mansion.

Finally, when the Lord says that He would go and prepare "a place" for us, He is referring to: a spot (generally in space, but limited by occupancy that is, location (as a position, home, tract of land, etc.). Jesus is saying that He is giving to us or preparing for us an excellent opportunity, or specifically a legal or licensed place, quarter, room, or building that we may occupy freely.

Those who choose Christ's salvation and Heaven will not be required to toil to pay rent. There will be no mortgages in our heavenly homes. Nor will we be required to till the ground to grow the food that we will eat. We will not be nourished by our own labors or the sweat of our brows. The implication is Paradise or Heaven, God's abode. Paul the apostle was also taken up or caught up into the realms of heaven and also saw Paradise. There is actually quite a bit of biblical evidence for these kinds of heavenly encounters or supernatural experiences. There are numerous examples of this throughout the Bible. Therefore, the kinds of experiences that are illustrated in this book are thoroughly biblical.

In John 14:1-6, Jesus is referring to the period of time after His resurrection. That is the hour that we live in now. It is only through the finished work of Christ and the atonement of Calvary that God forgave us and gave us this hope of accessing our heavenly home. It is only through the shed blood of Christ that covers humankind's sins that can we ascend into the heavens. Jesus said: *"I am the way, the truth, and the life. No one comes to the Father except through Me."* Jesus is the only legal means to access Heaven.

## JESUS IS THE KEY

This is a very important key to accessing these kinds of heavenly experiences and angelic visitations. We must come to the Father and to the Father's house or heavenly places through Christ. A person can access the realms of Heaven while they live upon the earth or in this temporal realm though spiritual experiences. Anyone can do this. Hopefully you will also access Heaven when you die and live in Heaven as an eternal spirit. However, as I taught in the second book of this trilogy, you can also access the realms of Heaven as a priest after the order of Melchizedek in this lifetime. You can visit Heaven now.

It was those kinds of experiences that radically transformed my life in the natural realm. When I would return to the earth from the heavenly realms, the grace and favor of God began to manifest in my life in an amazingly accelerated manner. When the reality of Christ's atonement became real to me, I began to understand the authenticity of who I am in Christ. The Lord initiated a metamorphosis within my life and circumstances. Jesus took me from sickness to health. He took me from hopelessness to happiness. The Messiah transformed my mindset and took me from poverty to prosperity in the natural realm. All of these wonderful blessings unfolded in my life in a supernaturally quick and efficient manner once I began to visit Heaven. Supernatural grace and favor with both God and man are the fruit of heavenly visitations.

I suppose that it could be said that the "fragrance of Heaven" attached itself to me, and when I returned to the earthly realms, my life was translated into a Kingdom of Heaven lifestyle. My mindset was renewed, and I began to think from a Christlike perspective—and that transformation of my mindset revolutionized every aspect of my life. This same Kingdom of Heaven is available to you too, and you can also have your life transformed and revolutionized in a similar, supernatural fashion.

The testimonies of angelic visitations and encounters that I shared in the first two books focused upon angelic encounters that occurred within the temporal realm. In other words, those angelic visitations occurred upon the earth, or within the earthly realm. For the most part, the angelic visitations and testimonies that I outlined in the first two books were examples of angelic visitations that happened in the natural realm. Those angelic encounters happened on earth and affected people's physical bodies. At times this resulted in the release of various kinds of miracles or healings. Many of those previous testimonies were what can be termed as "open eyed" angelic encounters.

Those angels were seen, felt, heard, smelled, tasted, or sensed and encountered by the person's five carnal senses. Some scholars call these the five traditional senses of the human body. In the testimonies of angelic visitations in this third book of the trilogy, we are going to examine angelic encounters that transpired in the spiritual realm—more specifically, in Heaven.

In the first two books of this trilogy, I expressed my belief that the Lord Jesus Christ was releasing His children to begin to co-labor with His angelic host in an accelerated manner. A few of the testimonies shared were taken from supernatural experiences where we encountered angels in the realms of Heaven. Some call these places the third heaven. No matter what terminology you choose to describe where these angelic encounters took place, the fact remains that these experiences were very real, life-changing, and they also give us glimpses into the realms of Heaven.

In book 2, I detailed how I was introduced to angels in a time of prayer by the Messiah. I described how I was taken into the very presence of Jesus as a new Christian. From the very beginning of my walk with Jesus, the supernatural aspects of the Lord have been evident in my life. The Lord used angelic ministry to trigger the reality of the supernatural characteristics of His Kingdom in my sphere of influence. The Lord employs angels to help my wife, Kathy, and me in our daily lives. Angels have helped establish our call and ministry. Angels are also active in many aspects of our lives including the areas of miracles, healings, as well as signs and wonders. Angels have moved mightily in protection, provision, and direction. We embrace God and angelic encounters; and angelic ministry has become a regular part of our daily lives! You can embrace angelic ministry, too.

## ENCOUNTERS, EXPERIENCES, VISIONS

I began to experience supernatural encounters almost immediately after I was saved. I saw these kinds of phenomena in the Bible, so I just expected them to happen in my life, too. I did not question the mystical or supernatural side of the Kingdom of Heaven. I was not brought up in the church; therefore, I was not indoctrinated to believe that the supernatural was to be looked upon with fear and suspicion. I assumed that these were just accepted and normal parts of Christ's Kingdom. I had not been religiously brainwashed, so I did not consider or take into account that visions and angelic encounters were not "supposed" to be routine parts of Christianity and walking with Jesus today. That is, according to most doctrine and churchy mindsets. I saw visions and angelic encounters in my old King James Bible—so I expected them as I walked with Christ.

Once I was praying and asking the Lord about my future in Him. I was certain that God had a purpose for me and a new direction for my life. I started to press into the Lord for an answer to this question by fasting and praying on a daily basis.

Soon I began to experience visions, or what some call third heaven encounters. Even as a babe in Christ I would embrace these phenomena; I simply thought these kinds of experiences were supposed to be normal as a Christian. In one such vision I "saw" Jesus clearly in the spirit. He was calling me to draw closer to Him. Jesus was holding out His arms, inviting and welcoming me to come into His presence. In my mind, I had a decision to make. Either I would go to Jesus, or I would dismiss this vision and continue to pray to Him in my little prayer closet. I chose to go to Him. Immediately I sensed that I was being catapulted through time and space. A short time later, I found myself in the very presence of Jesus Christ. This was my initial experience in heavenly places (see Eph. 1:3,20; 2:6). However, I soon discovered that when the Lord gave me the grace to ascend into His presence, His angels were always present in the heavenly realms around Jesus.

On that cold night back in back in 2001, as Jesus wrapped His arms around me, I was overcome by the knowledge of the powerful love He has for me. I also received a divine revelation of the unimaginable love that the Savior has for every person upon the planet Earth. The Messiah desperately loves every tongue, tribe, and nation. God loves Jew and Gentile alike. Jesus has a very special place in His heart and a burning passion for the Jewish people from which His heritage springs. The Messiah desperately desires for all of the Jewish people to fully understand His Kingdom. The future will hold a wonderful time of the fulfillment of this desire of Jesus' heart, and the Jew and the Gentile will become one in the Messiah (see Eph. 2:14-22).

## I AM CALLING YOU

On that night Jesus said that He was going to tell me who I am. This, of course, was an answer to my ongoing prayers. Jesus said, "Kevin, I am calling you to be an artist, an author, and evangelist." The words Jesus spoke to me penetrated to the very depth of my being. The Lord held me for a long time, and I wept uncontrollably in His arms of love. When I stepped back from the Lord, I saw that He was flanked by four strong angels. These enchanting creatures seemed to be overjoyed in the fact that I was standing in the very presence of Jesus. The angels welcomed me, and they smiled at me with assurance.

Jesus moved His right hand in a sweeping motion indicating the four angels that were present. He said, "Today I am assigning these angels to your ministry." I was a new believer. This statement baffled me, as I had no ministry. Just as quickly as it began, the experience was over. However, the feeling of Christ's supernatural love and presence rested upon me for days after that heavenly encounter. When the vision ended, I found myself back in my prayer closet weeping greatly. I continued to weep every time this vision came into my mind for several months.

A few days later I was praying when I saw Jesus again. He was requesting me to come to Him for a second time. I was ready to go without hesitation. I experienced the same sensation of being launched and could feel my spirit being sucked out of my body. I came to rest in the very presence of Jesus, and He was flanked by the same four angels. I fell to my knees and began to weep once again as I felt the power of His unconditional love. Two of the angels moved to my side and helped me to stand. Then Jesus looked deeply and lovingly into my eyes. Jesus placed His nail-scarred hands upon my shoulders and told me that He was assigning the first of the four angels to me at that moment. This was the beginning of an extended season of heavenly visitations for me.

During this special time, one of the angels stepped forward. This angel was about seven and a half feet tall and had long, golden locks of beautiful hair that cascaded onto his broad shoulders. I could not help but notice the power and peace that my new friend carried with his countenance. This helped to relax me and put me at ease with the unfolding events. Then the angel that the Lord was speaking of smiled at me, and I gazed into his beautiful sky blue eyes for a moment as I listened to Jesus speaking to me. Jesus told me that He was assigning this angel of protection and provision to me at that moment. My mind raced as I wondered what it meant to have an angel assigned to me. The Lord told me the angel's name and his function or anointing. The Lord also explained to me how I could activate this angel to work on my behalf, or for the benefit of others. This angel is empowered by the Lord to grant and release provision and protection. You may be interested to know that you also have angels assigned to you with similar abilities (see Ps. 91:11).

Since that encounter I have never doubted the existence of the Lord's angelic beings nor their constant intervention in my life. When I finished working on the first book, *Dancing with Angels 1,* the Holy Spirit spoke to me that one of the omitted chapters entitled Angels in Heaven was meant to be sculpted into an entire book. I was instantly given heavenly revelation concerning those testimonies. They had been recorded and kept over the past decade. I realized that these early heavenly experiences, which the Lord had instructed me to write down, would give people wonderful glimpses and insights into the realms of Heaven. People would be able to have a better understanding of the very heart of God. It was from those testimonies of angelic encounters in the heavenly realms that this book was birthed.

I am convinced that these testimonies will bring a smile to your face and joy into your heart as you read them. Kathy and I hope that you enjoy them and find these tiny portraits of the heart of God the Father, God the Son, and God the Holy Spirit, and the heavenly places inspiring to your faith in God. A passage from Ephesians outlines these possibilities for our lives as we live and breathe in Christ:

> *God, who is rich in mercy, because of His great love with which He loved us, even when we were dead in trespasses, made us alive together with Christ (by grace you have been saved), and raised us up together, and made us sit together in the heavenly places in Christ Jesus, that in the ages to come He might show the exceeding riches of His grace in His kindness toward us in Christ Jesus. For by grace you have been saved through faith, and that not of yourselves; it is the gift of God* (Ephesians 2:4-8).

It is important to lay a more sure foundation concerning the testimonies that I will share with you in the coming pages. Therefore, in an attempt to clarify the reality of angelic ministry and the legitimacy of these kinds of heavenly experiences I will work to build on the foundation that has been laid in this Prologue in the next section of this book. Lord willing, this will help give you more insight to these supernatural testimonies as we examine them through the lens of the Scriptures.

## ENDNOTES

1. Strong's Greek Concordance #G3614.

2. See Romans 11, 8:14,19, 9:26, Galatians 3:26, 4:6.

3. See Strong's Greek Concordance reference #G3306.

4. See Strong's Greek Concordance reference #G5117.

5. See 2 Corinthians 12:1-3, Ezekiel 1:1, Revelation 4:1, Genesis 28:12, and Genesis 32:2 to name but a few.

# THE ASSIGNMENT OF ANGELS

As I HAVE SAID, ANGELIC visitations can transpire in one of two realms. We can have angelic visitations in the earthly or temporal realm—the natural realm we live in. We contact that realm with our five carnal senses. We can say that we interact with the temporal realm through our soul, which is made up of our mind, will, and emotions. We also relate to the earthly realm or the earthly environment through our bodies or flesh. As we press into the Kingdom of God, we will begin to experience segments of time when our spirit will become dominant in terms of perception. By the way, when I say "press into the Kingdom of God," I am referring to seeking the Lord with all of our hearts.

When we seek the Lord with all of our spirits, souls, and bodies, the Lord promises that we will find Him (see Jer. 29:11-14, Matt. 6:33, John 14:21). The Scriptures also tell us that we can violently seek the Kingdom of God. That is what launched me into these heavenly realms of Christ's Kingdom. It was my passion and hunger to know Jesus Christ in a more intimate and tangible way. Your passion and hunger can also open the door of the heavens to you, too. I believe that anyone can have these kinds of supernatural experiences. It is even possible that the testimonies in this book can become a prophetic word for you (see Rev. 19:10).

There can be instances and periods when the Lord will call many of us to storm the gates of Heaven and to take the Kingdom by force. Again, this is what I mean when I speak of "pressing in." Really, it is just a matter of allowing the Holy Spirit to develop a holy hunger within you. Matthew 11:12 illustrates this point: *"And from the days of John the Baptist until now the kingdom of heaven suffers violence, and the violent take it by force."* Sometimes you need to take the Kingdom of Heaven by force!

## THE VERY IMAGE OF JESUS

We are created in the very image of the Creator of the heavens and the earth. We see this spelled out in Genesis 1:26, *"Then God said, "Let Us make man in Our image, according to Our likeness."* The Bible clearly teaches us that God is a spiritual being who is made up of three parts. This aspect of the Lord's nature is commonly referred to as the Trinity, composed of God the Father, God the Son, and God the Holy Spirit. Likewise, you are also created by the Lord as a triune being. You have a spirit, a soul, and a body.

Apostle Paul understood this three-part composition of people and encourages us in First Thessalonians 5:23 in connection with this dynamic of our spiritual nature: *"Now may the God of peace Himself sanctify you completely; and may your whole spirit, soul, and body be preserved blameless at the coming of our Lord Jesus Christ."* Paul shares foundational truths in this Scripture pertaining to how the Lord created us as a three-part being. Paul encouraged us concerning our responsibility to grow and mature as the Lord's children, just as human babies are created to grow into adults.

Each person has a spirit. Our spirit is the "real" person of our existence, and it is our spirit that is regenerated, or "born again," at the moment that we pray to receive the salvation of the Messiah. Our spirit is at the core of our being. Your spirit is the "real you." And it is your spirit that is actually born again and will live on in eternity with Christ in Heaven.

Each person has a soul. Our soul is made up of our mind, will, and emotions. For most of us, our soul rules our daily lives. For the most part, we live our lives allowing our souls to dominate our daily activities and choices. In other words, we allow our intellect—mind, will, and emotions—to rule and reign in our daily lives and day-to-day decisions.

Each person has a body, too. This, of course, is our flesh. Most people in the world are ruled by their fleshly desires. We all have basic needs each day such as food, clothing, and shelter. The carnal desires of our flesh are powerful driving forces behind most humans' lives. This is true for the majority of Christians, too. Most born-again people never really achieve the victory that the Messiah purchased for us on the cross. Many people struggle through life. The primary reason for this is because we allow our soul—mind, will, and emotions—and our flesh to rule our lives. Few of us are really led by our spirit.

Apostle Paul referred to Christians like this as "carnal Christians". In other words, people can receive Jesus Christ as Savior, and yet never really mature into the fullness of Christ's salvation (see 1 Cor. 3:1-4). As we saw in First Thessalonians 5:23, Paul encourages you and I to be sanctified completely—spirit, soul, and body. Paul clearly delineates from the three aspects of our created nature.

We need to allow the precious Holy Spirit to transform us. Scriptures tell us that we need to seek to have our minds (our souls) transformed or sanctified. Ephesians 4:22-24 outlines this Kingdom dynamic for us:

> *Put off...your former conduct, the old man which grows corrupt according to the deceitful lusts, and be renewed in the spirit of your mind, and that you put on the new man which was created according to God, in true righteousness and holiness.*

This Scripture in Ephesians 4 tells us that it is our responsibility to overcome or to put off the corrupt conduct and deceitful lusts that are evident in our flesh. In other words we are instructed to bring our flesh into subjection to our regenerated or reborn spirits. In addition to this, we are to renew our mind. This also deals with the transformation of our soulish nature, carnal nature, or worldly mindsets. Paul is referring to the sanctifying of our soul and the reformation of our flesh. Only as we mature and begin to bring our soul and flesh into submission to our spirit can we begin to enter and entertain the spiritual aspects of Christ's Kingdom in fullness. Some folks call this dynamic sanctification, or walking in holiness.

It is important to understand that we have a part to play in this process of sanctification. We need to renew our minds according to the admonitions of Paul found in Romans 12:1-2:

> *I beseech you therefore, brethren, by the mercies of God, that you present your bodies a living sacrifice, holy, acceptable to God, which is your reasonable service. And do not be conformed to this world, but be transformed by the renewing of your mind, that you may prove what is that good and acceptable and perfect will of God.*

Paul instructs us that it is our reasonable service to have our minds renewed. We are also instructed to bring our flesh into submission to God in holiness. That part is up to us. God does not promise to do that for us in His Word. Unfortunately, very few people actually realize the need for sanctification, and fewer still seek to implement the process of restoration and renewing of their minds, which again is an element of our soul. We can help activate the process of renewing our minds by washing our minds, will, and emotions with the power and anointing of God's Word. So as we study God's Word and meditate upon God's Word in our minds (the driving force of our souls), we will be renewed and transformed into a Christlike nature. Our souls (mind, will, and, emotions) will become Christlike, and we will learn to be led by the Holy Spirit constantly. We will grow into the very nature and character of Jesus.

As this supernatural process begins to unfold in our lives, we will mature in Christ and initiate our transformation into His image and character. Once this happens we will be able to minister in the anointing of Jesus found in Hebrews 4:14, *"we have a great High Priest who has passed through the heavens, Jesus the Son of God, let us hold fast our confession."*

## SEEK REVELATION, AUTHORITY, AND POWER

We will begin to understand that we too can pass through the heavens to seek revelation, authority, and power from the very throne of God. In other words, we will begin to minister in the anointing or the mantle of Melchizedek. We will be transformed into Christlikeness and then we will represent Christ in our spheres of influence and become priests forever according to the order of Melchizedek. We will have the ability to recognize aspects from the spiritual realm and, as the Lord allows and gives us grace, actually demonstrate the ability to pass through the heavens and enter into the very presence of God—just like Christ.

Scripture tells us that it is possible for you and me to mature and to grow up into the very nature and character of Jesus Christ. As we submit to this process, we will begin to see our very nature transformed. Our three-part or triune nature will begin to be turned inside out. Instead of being ruled and led by our soul and our flesh, we can be changed in a moment and in the twinkle of an eye. We will be led by our "real selves" or our spirits. Romans 8:14 tells us that *"For as many as are led by the Spirit of God, these are sons of God."* As children of God, our spirits can become dominant for segments of time. Our spirits can become dominant for a few seconds. Our spirits can become dominate, in terms of perception, for a few minutes, or even a few days. That is what I believe happened to me during the season I experienced the visitations into the heavenly realms that are documented in this book.

When this process begins to accelerate in our lives, we will begin to perceive attributes from the spiritual realm much more clearly than we did when we were driven by our carnal mind, intellect, soul, and flesh in terms of our perception. We will begin to perceive the spiritual realm in a much greater way, and the eyes of our spiritual understanding will be enlightened or opened to see, hear, taste, touch, and enter into the Kingdom of Heaven. This has been called the "seer anointing." Of course, Jesus was our role model for this. I have outlined this aspect of Christ's mission and ministry on the earth in great detail in the second book of this trilogy.

Jesus shed His blood to make you and I kings and priests who would have the authority and the supernatural ability to have the eyes of our understanding enlightened; that we might understand the hope of His calling for each of us so we would comprehend the riches of the glory of our inheritance. That we might know the exceeding greatness of His power toward each of us who believe, through the working of His mighty power, which the Father worked in Christ when He raised Him from the dead and seated Him at His right hand in the heavenly places. Thus also allowing you and I to have these same supernatural privileges by blazing a trail and making a way for us to be seated at God's right hand in the heavenly places far above all principality, power, might, dominion, and every name that is named among men. That is our calling and inheritance—and we can step into it in this lifetime (see Eph. 1:18-20, Rev. 1:5-6; 5:9-10).

However, I wanted to briefly outline these Kingdom principles here so you will be aware that there are seasons in our lives when we can be led more so by our regenerated or reborn spirits than by our mind, will, emotions, and our flesh. It is during such times that the temporal realm becomes secondary to us in terms of perception. We will begin to perceive more dominantly with our spirits and the eyes of our hearts, or spiritual senses. At these times we will begin to see and experience the reality of the spiritual Kingdom of God in a great and mighty way. Our spirits will perceive the reality of the spiritual realm in a dominate fashion. Really, this dynamic is the spiritual gift of discerning of spirits that activates in our lives when we become born again, or reborn from the heavenly realms (see 1 Cor. 12:10).

# HEAVEN IS REAL!

During these instances of time, we will begin to have supernatural experiences, such as angelic visitations. We can begin to interact with the Kingdom of Heaven and experience trances, visions, and other supernatural encounters with Christ's Kingdom. Occasionally, we will be given grace to actually be taken into heavenly realms to interact with Christ, His Kingdom, God's angelic beings, and various places found there. That is what this book is all about. It is an illustration of the reality of the spiritual Kingdom of Heaven. This book paints a portrait of Heaven through the eyes of a person who walked out this dynamic over an extended period of time. Of course this is only possible by the grace of God. Isn't it a wonderful blessing that God gives us all His grace freely?

I will share numerous testimonies with you of times when I was given the grace to actually ascend into the heavenly realms and to be seated with Christ Jesus in heavenly places. It could be accurately said that I was taken into Heaven by God's Spirit and allowed to return to the earth in order to document the places, things, and culture of heavenly realms that I saw there.

Heaven is real! You have a future and a heavenly home waiting for you if you are God's child. I pray that this book will encourage you and give you a glimpse of what your heavenly home will look like. I pray that it will encourage you to draw closer to Jesus.

Apostle Paul had similar experiences. In Second Corinthians 12:2, Paul testifies of these kinds of supernatural experiences saying:

> *I know a man in Christ who fourteen years ago—whether in the body I do not know, or whether out of the body I do not know, God knows—such a one was caught up to the third heaven.*

Paul tells us that he was unsure of whether he was actually in his body or out of his body when he was taken up into the third heaven. I am not certain either, but what I am sure of is that the visions and experiences that I lived through and that I document in this book are real. It is possible that I was taken into the very realms of Heaven. I saw places in Heaven, and I share those with you in this book. My prayer is that these testimonies will reveal the heart of God and His everlasting love to you.

I am also sure that during this season my spirit became dominate in terms of perception. This, along with the grace and favor of God, was certainly responsible for the precious privilege of walking with Jesus in the realms of Heaven. The Lord Jesus Himself requested me to write these testimonies of Heaven that are recorded and documented in this book. He even spoke to me while I was in Heaven one day and gave me instructions as to how I was to actually acquire a personal computer to use as I wrote and documented these supernatural events. Within 48 hours after Jesus told me how to get a computer to document these heavenly visitations, I had the PC He had told me about in the heavenly realms, sitting on the kitchen table in my little house at 121 Beech Street in Bluefield, West Virginia. Most of the testimonies that are documented in this book were written using that old personal computer in that season between 2001 and 2002.

Having said all of this in the hope of laying a foundation for these heavenly testimonies, let's begin our miraculous journey together into the heart of God and the realms of Heaven.

## THE MARRIAGE SUPPER

One of the first places that the Lord allowed me to explore the heavenly realms is a wonderful place that I call the great banquet hall. I invested many hours fellowshipping with Jesus in this great room. Perhaps it will be a room such as this where we will, Lord willing, partake of the wedding supper of the Lamb of God. In the epilogue we look at what may be such a place which the apostle John documented in Revelation 19:1-9:

> *After these things I heard a loud voice of a great multitude in heaven, saying, "Alleluia! Salvation and glory and honor and power belong to the Lord our God! For true and righteous are*

*His judgments, because He has judged the great harlot who cor-*
*rupted the earth with her fornication; and He has avenged on*
*her the blood of His servants shed by her." Again they said, "Alle-*
*luia! Her smoke rises up forever and ever!" And the twenty-four*
*elders and the four living creatures fell down and worshiped*
*God who sat on the throne, saying, "Amen! Alleluia!" Then a*
*voice came from the throne, saying, "Praise our God, all you*
*His servants and those who fear Him, both small and great!"*
*And I heard, as it were, the voice of a great multitude, as the*
*sound of many waters and as the sound of mighty thunderings,*
*saying, "Alleluia! For the Lord God Omnipotent reigns! Let us*
*be glad and rejoice and give Him glory, for the marriage of the*
*Lamb has come, and His wife has made herself ready." And to*
*her it was granted to be arrayed in fine linen, clean and bright,*
*for the fine linen is the righteous acts of the saints. Then he said*
*to me, "Write: 'Blessed are those who are called to the marriage*
*supper of the Lamb!'" And he said to me, "These are the true*
*sayings of God."*

One thing is for sure. Heaven will be a wonderful and lively place to live in comfort for eternity!

In the first chapter, you will travel to the great banquet hall with me and meet the Messiah in person. It was in that place that I invested many days just lying at the feet of Jesus. I was not speaking, not striving; I was just resting in the presence of the Lord. From those encounters in the heavenly realms, my life was transformed and the grace and favor of God seemed to permeate my very being. I pray that same anointing will also permeate your life spirit, soul, and body as you read the following testimonies of Heaven and of God's angels therein. I pray that the subsequent testimonies will become prophetic promises for you personally (see Rev. 19:10).

The following chapters document dozens of visits with the Lord in the heavenly places. It never occurred to me to write these experiences down, and I did I not have any intention to do so. I had purposed to keep them treasured within my heart. I would not have written any of this had it not been for the Lord instructing me to do so during this season. Let me share with you the things that Jesus showed me in the heavenly places during that season. These testimonies will give you a wonderful portrait of the heart of the Lord, and you will also learn how Heaven appears. In Chapter 1, we will explore the Father's house.

# The Genesis

S HORTLY AFTER I WAS INVITED to ascend into the very presence of Jesus, my life began to radically change. As you may recall, I was seeking the Lord in prayer when Jesus appeared to me in a vision and invited me to come to Him. At that moment, I was unaware that it was actually possible to ascend from the earth and really enter into the very presence of Jesus in the heavenly realms. After that initial experience, visions, or what some call heavenly encounters, unfolded in my life on a regular basis.

At this point in my life I was still struggling from the consequences of my sin and iniquity. So I was still living in poverty, sickness, oppression, and daily battling addiction. I was not using drugs, but the desire to relapse was a constant temptation. I was working and sought to pray every waking moment in this season. I could not wait to finish work each day so I could return to the little house at 121 Beech Street and enter into my prayer closet. More often than not, I would experience supernatural encounters; and for a season, I was regularly allowed to ascend into the heavenly realms. I soon discovered that when the Lord gave me the grace to ascend into His presence, His angels were always present in the heavenly realms around Him.

After that cold night back in early 2001 when Jesus wrapped His arms around me, I became totally convinced of the reality of Christ's Kingdom and His will for me to interact with Him in the heavens. That is Christ's desire for you, too. That is your supernatural inheritance (see 1 Peter 1:3-4). I would rush home from work and often immediately enter into the tangible presence of the Lord. Some theologians call this kind of the weighty presence of the Lord the *shekinah* glory of God.

It seemed that the person of the Holy Spirit was often waiting for me to unlock the front door and walk in. There were even times when I would open the front door and the power of God would be so strong in the small living room that I would fall out under the power of the Holy Spirit. I would lay prostrate on the floor for hours. Other times I would return home to the little house at 121 Beech Street and quickly clean my body from a day of painting. Then I would position myself in prayer in my prayer closet—my five by eight foot bathroom. Often during this season I would be taken up into the heavens to have encounters and visitations with Jesus.

These kinds of experiences in the heavenly realms were simply a continuation of the supernatural encounters and visitations of Jesus and His angels I wrote about in *Dancing with Angels 1*. The main difference in these heavenly experiences was that I was encountering the Lord and His Kingdom in my own home. By the grace of God, I succeeded in opening the heavens over my life. I recount this process and give you step by step directions to repeat this supernatural procedure in my previous books.

The visitations shared in this book were initiated in the temporal or carnal realm but progressed into the heavenly realm. These experiences went on consistently for more than nine months. I would daily ascend into the realms of Heaven and fellowship with the Lord Jesus. Often He would take me to different places in the Heaven. It was a wonderful and life-changing time. In the natural realm I was poor, oppressed, and struggling greatly. But spiritually I was blessed with every spiritual blessing in the heavenly places, just as Ephesians 1:3 describes, *"Blessed be the God and Father of our Lord Jesus Christ, who has blessed us with every spiritual blessing in the heavenly places in Christ.*" In the temporal or natural realm I was poor and oppressed; but in the spiritual realm, I was a truly blessed billionaire (see Luke 6:20)!

## HIS PRESENCE

After the night in the heavenly realms when Jesus called me to be an artist, an author, and evangelist, the level and the grace of God greatly multiplied in my life and within my personal sphere of influence. I have written about how the Lord supernaturally prospered me through the activation and release of angelic ministry. This served to open doors for me to travel around the earth and do the work of an evangelist. Those events are discussed in *Dancing with Angels 1* and *2*. However, during that whole period of time I was consistently having experiences where I would be allowed to be taken up into Heaven in various ways to sit in the presence of Jesus. I will share some of those testimonies in the next few chapters. On many days and nights during this season I chose to just lie at the feet of Jesus and breathe in His presence. Christ was my portion (see Ps. 16:5). One single moment in the presence of Jesus can be life changing.

The Lord was almost always accompanied by the same four strong angels that He had introduced to me the first time I went to Him in prayer. These angelic friends always seemed to be delighted by the fact that I was able to come into the very presence of Jesus in the heavenly places. They always welcomed me; I have seen them many times over the past decade, both in the heavens and also upon the earth. I know these angels of God well. The Lord had said with a sweeping motion of His right hand, "Today I am assigning these four angels to your ministry." Those four angels have helped Kathy and me minister in many ways, in many nations, and to many people over the years.

After that experience, as I was praying when I saw Jesus again, He was requesting me to come to Him for a second time. I was ready to go without hesitation. I experienced the same sensation of being launched and could feel my spirit being sucked out of my body. I came to rest in the very presence of Jesus, and He was flanked by the same four angels. Almost daily over the course of the next several months I was given the grace to experience similar types of supernatural trips and translations into the heavenly realms. Again, ever since those earliest encounters I have never doubted the existence of the Lord's angelic beings nor their constant intervention in my life. God's angels surely intervene in your life and circumstances too, although you may not be aware of them.

## An Intimate and Personal Relationship

In fact, the Lord continues to allow me to ascend into the heavenly realms at times. During these experiences, I am often shown events and situations that will unfold upon the earth, or within a ministry situation. However, from the very beginning of these trips to Heaven, one of my favorite places to visit is the great banquet hall.

The first several dozen times that I walked with the Lord in Heaven, I always met Him first in the great banquet hall and dined with the Messiah there. Then Jesus would take me out into the realms of the Father's heavenly creation and show me various places and things there. Those trips will constitute the majority of the material in this book, and I hope that you enjoy the descriptions of Heaven that I share with you.

Beginning in 2001, I began to make regular excursions into the great banquet hall to meet the Messiah. As I stated earlier, for a season that lasted about nine months, I visited Heaven almost on a daily basis. Here is how these supernatural excursions began. After I had returned from Canada, I was totally transformed. All of the experiences that I shared in *Dancing with Angels 1* and *Dancing with Angels 2* had transformed my mindset. I was not content to have a "normal" form of Christianity any longer. Attending church one day a week was not enough for me.

I desperately desired to have an intimate relationship with God. I soon discovered that the Creator of Heaven and earth desperately desired to have an intimate and personal relationship with me, too. I realized that there was more to Christ and His Kingdom—and I wanted it all. I would lay upon my bed and meditate upon the times that I had been taken up into the realms of Heaven—like the night near Bay Roberts, Canada, when I had walked with the Lord for hours in the heavenly realms by the sea of glass like crystal (see Rev. 4:6).

I would think about how the passion and love of Jesus had touched me deep inside on November 25, 2001, in Springdale, Newfoundland. I had seen the heavens open and the angels of the Lord that evening. Later I had been visited by Jesus, and the Lord had personally called me to declare the Gospel of the Kingdom. Jesus had touched my left hand and commissioned me into the nations of the earth to preach and minister the Word of God, telling me that He would be with me everywhere I would go. Over the years this statement has been proven true as I have seen the Lord in many nations while traveling and preaching. I have seen the Lord show up as I was ministering in Tanzania, India, Italy, England, Singapore, and Ecuador, to name a few.

However, when I returned to the United States, these kind of supernatural experiences dried up, and it seemed that the heavens were bronze over my head (see Deut. 28:23). I was not experiencing the same kind of intimacy with the Holy Spirit like I had encountered on Killick Island on the Bay of Exploits. I purposed in my heart to storm the gates of Heaven until I drew close to the Lord once again. I was desperate to touch the hem of His garment. I longed to have real communion with the Person of the Holy Spirit once again. I fasted and prayed for a long time until I got the breakthrough.

## PORTAL OF GLORY

One day I prepared myself to enter into my little prayer room. It seemed like just another day. I lay down on the old shag carpet that I had put on the floor. I prayed and repented for everything that I could think of. Then I just purposed to wait upon the Lord. After a while, I began to feel a sensation of ascending. In my spirit, I could feel myself being drawn upward. When I opened my eyes, I could see my body lying on the carpet in the little house below. I continued to accelerate upward, and it seemed as if my vision switched to hyper-speed; I entered into a tunnel of sorts leaving the earth below.

The tunnel or portal was made up of light, and I seemed to be traveling through it at the speed of sound. The sensation was quite remarkable. I relaxed and purposed within my heart to enjoy the ride. I began to look at the walls of light that compromised the tunnel. The colors were amazing, reminding me of how the tiny snowflakes had phosphoresced and supernaturally reflected the sunlight on Killick Island. It was a thrilling sight, and I became engrossed in examining the walls of light on the tunnel as I was accelerating upward. I could feel my body twisting and turning much like you might experience if you were riding a roller coaster on earth. I twisted and turned and accelerated skyward at the speed of sound for a long time.

Unexpectedly there was an ethereal light at the end of the tunnel. Suddenly the tunnel began to turn downward and I slid out the end of the tunnel in much the same way that you would slip off a tall sliding board into a swimming pool. For an instant my vision was blurry, and I landed upon my hands and knees. I gasped for air, but I was not injured at all. I looked down at my hands and noticed that I was kneeling upon smooth stones. The joints of the stones were impeccably joined and there was no mortar in the cracks. I could smell the pungent fragrances of flowers and the smell of frankincense filled my nose. I was wondering where I was when I felt two pairs of strong hands lift me up to a standing position.

## ANGELIC WELCOME

On my left and right were two angels. They were smiling at me and welcoming me to this place. I looked at each one in turn and realized that these were two of the four angels that Jesus had assigned to me earlier. Both angels were gazing at me benevolently; I had a knowing that they were very glad I was with them. I also knew that I was in the heavenly places. A gentle breeze ruffled my hair, and I took my first look at Heaven.

I was standing upon a beautiful stone pathway. In my mind I purposed in my heart to look at these stones in more detail later, because of the amazing craftsmanship needed to create them. I could see manicured grounds and what seemed to be an endless sea of fields, orchards, and well-tended rose gardens that covered the land nearby. The fragrance I was experiencing was wafting up from the incredibly beautiful botanical gardens. They stretched out for miles before me. In the distance I saw a beautiful, crystal clear river meandering peacefully through the gardens. I wondered if there were any bass in the river, and I had the desire to hike down to it one day.

Glancing to my left I saw a massive stone home situated perfectly upon a peak. I noticed that the stone pathway I was standing on led to the entrance of the home, or what may have actually been a castle. In perfect luminosity, the stone castle reflected the radiance of the ethereal light of this place. In fact, the castle seemed to glow in the evening sunshine at that precise moment. The house seemed to be beckoning to me in the spirit.

I could hear harps and stringed instruments worshiping, and I was certain that the music was coming from the open arched windows of the home. Suddenly I realized that the music was the same as what I had heard when the heavens had opened in Canada. I could hear angelic singing, but was unable to understand the language of the songs. It seemed that I had been frozen in time, yet only a few seconds had transpired since I had landed on the pathway.

I looked at the two angels a second time to see them gently smiling at me. The angel holding my left arm released his grip and pointed at the stone castle. It was about four hundred feet above me and about a quarter mile away. I could see that the stone pathway led in the direction of the castle. I understood that I should walk to it. I took a few steps on the smooth, light-colored stones; and for the first time, I could feel the coolness of them on the soles of my bare feet. It was refreshing and surprising at the same time. I looked down and noticed that I was barefooted. I turned to look at the two angels again and saw them wave goodbye to me. They smiled and turned to walk in the opposite direction on the pathway.

## UP TOWARD THE CASTLE

I understood that they had other chores to do. Had the pair of angels come to welcome me, or perhaps they actually played a role in transporting me to this place? After all, I had once been taken up into the heavenly places by an angel that dropped me off in the very presence of Jesus.

Thinking about this made me smile, and I turned to gaze at the manicured gardens below. Once again the wind tousled my hair, and the pleasant aromas of this place assaulted my sense of smell, causing the smile on my face to expand. I enjoyed these new smells as I walked about on the stone pathway leading toward the castle. As I walked, I listened carefully to the worship that filled the air in this place. It was delightful. On earth we would call it anointed, and it seemed to be tangible. Although I could not understand the words, I knew that the lyrics glorified the Lamb of God. This also made my heart leap with joy.

After a short while, I came to a place where the pathway diverged. One part led down the knoll to the hundreds of manicured gardens. From this vantage point I could see what looked like a circular fountain, and beyond that the crystal clear river flowed through the middle of the gardens. I knew that it was the presence of the river that gave the plants and gardens their source of life and helped them bear much fruit.

I had a strong desire to walk down to the gardens, but I knew I was supposed to visit the castle first. Off to my left, obscured by flowery vines and other foliage, was a stone walkway that led to a perfectly positioned set of stairs. The beautiful flowering vines released a pungent fragrance similar to honeysuckle. The wonderful bouquet of the flowers swirled thickly in the air near a gate. They were brilliantly colored crimson and purple flowers that almost obscured the entrance and the metal gate. The gate was fashioned of what appeared to be precious metals, which surprised me. On earth, few gates are welded together using gold, silver, platinum, and other precious metals. I had to move the flowering vines to reach the gate with my right hand. As I opened the small polished gate, the sun reflected off the material sending colors flying into the air. I walked through, closed the gate behind me, and began to climb the stairs.

The stairway was flanked by two stone walls that were topped with perfectly smooth and joined stones. Once again I wondered about the precision of the craftsmanship that was used in the construction of these walls and stairs. There was no mortar visible, and the stones seemed to be joined perfectly together in some sort of supernatural manner. As I walked up the stairway, I stopped from time to time at small flat landings and looked out onto the gardens and the river below. These flat spots seemed to be rest areas that had been purposely incorporated into the design of the stairway. I rested my hands upon the smooth stones and gazed out at Heaven. Occasionally, I could feel tiny plants beneath my hands, so I stooped to look at them. I was astonished to see very tiny flowers growing on plants that spilled artfully over the polished stones.

These miniature flowers were the most beautiful shade of purple I had ever seen. It occurred to me that these were not random but rather had been specifically placed there by a master gardener. I spent a long time looking at them individually and stooped to smell their aroma. It was amazing that such a small group of flowers could have such a concentrated scent. This Scripture came into my mind, *"Solomon in all his glory was not arrayed like one of these"* (Matt. 6:29). I am certain that everything on earth is merely a reflection of the reality of Heaven. This thought also made me smile, and it leaped within my spirit with great joy.

I continued my supernatural trek up the secret stairway. I found myself in awe of my surroundings and the obvious attention to detail that was characteristic of this miraculous place.

When I reached the top of the stairway, I came to a large, oval balcony. It was perfectly positioned to allow a spectacular view of the landscape and gardens below. I walked over to lean against the stone wall there and continued to gaze out upon the beautiful countryside below. This was God's country. Within my heart I desired to visit those places someday. With so many incredible places to go to see, it would take me an eternity to investigate and explore them all, especially the places that looked to be promising and prime fishing spots along the river. I made a mental note to bring my rod and reel, if possible, on my next trip here. This thought caused a chuckle to bubble up from within my spirit, and a smile once again divided my face. Pure joy enveloped me at that instant.

I lingered there for a long time taking in the view. All the while angelic worship filled my ears and the fragrances of Heaven wafted into my nose from below. I became lost in my thoughts and time without end seemed to pass me by. The evening sun began to descend, and when it reached a perfect angle, the river below exploded with glorious light bringing my mind back to my present circumstances.

I heard a soft sound coming from behind me, and I turned to see what it was.

# CHAPTER 2

# THE FATHER'S HOUSE

I turned to see a pair of ancient doors set into the walls of the castle on the balcony. These were remarkably large and hinged in what appeared to be gold. There were also two large circular handles, one on each door. At that moment the door on the left opened. A large angel stepped out and motioned me to enter. He had golden brown hair and was powerful, yet he had a kind and compassionate smile. It seemed that he, too, had been expecting me.

I crossed the fifty feet from the wall to the two massive doors. As I passed through the door, for the first time I noticed how old and large they actually were. They appeared to be about twenty-five feet tall. These doors were impeccably maintained and preserved even though they appeared to be ageless. Yet as the angel closed the door, the hinges glided freely and silently. The thought came to me that there must be a wonderfully talented carpenter in this place. This amazed me. I stepped through into a very long hallway.

Inside the castle it was bright, but I did not see any light fixtures. The angel took a position to the right of the door and stood at attention. I looked down the hallway that looked to be hundreds of feet long. The sound of the angelic worship was louder now, and the fragrance of frankincense and myrrh was tangible and thick in this place. The stones below my feet were cool and smooth, just like the ones outside. I turned once more to look at the angel—a gatekeeper of sorts. When I looked into the angel's eyes, this Scripture came into my mind, *"Bless the LORD, all you servants of the Lord, who by night stand in the house of the Lord"* (Ps. 134:1). As this thought passed through my mind, the angel's smile brightened, and I realized that I should walk down the hall.

## SHIELDS OF FAITH

As I moved on, I noticed the height and breadth of the hallway, and I understood that even though it was just a hall it was a very special place. The ceilings were very high and vaulted. The architecture in the stone castle was amazing. As I strolled down the hall, I noticed shiny shields flanking me on each side of the walls. At first I thought that it was odd to see these shields displayed in the hallway. However, as I walked passed one, I realized that these were masterpieces. The shields were extremely valuable works of art. At once I understood that these shields were the actual shields of faith belonging to some of the Bible's greatest heroes and patriarchs. I saw the shield of King David. It was beautiful; yet I could clearly see the dents and marks of battle. The shields of Gideon, Samuel, and Rahab were also on display.

I stopped and examined closely some of these as I walked slowly down the hall. There were dozens, even hundreds of these shields of faith in the hallway. It also occurred to me that the majority of the shields that were on display were the shields of faith of God's friends. What was surprising to me was that many were the shields of faith of men and women the people of earth will never know. These are ordinary people whom the Lord treasures greatly. Their faith is an actual substance, and in the heavenly realms, that is extremely valuable to the Lord (see Heb. 11:1).

God takes great pleasure in the faith of ordinary men and women who place their trust and confidence totally in Him. As this understanding bubbled up from within my spirit, I knew this was an aspect of the rest of the Lord; trusting God. That is true faith. Such faith is pleasing to God the Father. In fact, without such faith it is impossible to please the Lord. Surely, God will reward such faith because that kind of faith is Kingdom faith. It is real, and it is tangible in the spiritual or heavenly realms (see Heb. 11:6). True faith is more valuable in Heaven than platinum, gold, silver, or even fine gemstones like rubies and diamonds. My stroll down this hallway turned out to be an epiphany—an "ah hah" moment.

I had been walking down the hallway observing these shields of faith for more than an hour when I realized that I had only gone about one-tenth of the way down the hall! In the center of the hallway ahead I could see a lot of light coming into the space from the right side, and I thought that the hall must open to a courtyard at that point. At that moment another angel stepped into the hallway and motioned me to enter into a room on the left.

## A Time of Refreshing

When I stepped through the threshold of the door, I realized that I had stepped into a magnificent bathroom. Unlike the hallway, the floors here were made of immaculate white marble, as were the walls. The room was filled with brilliant light as sunshine flowed into the space through a large twelve-foot circular window that was set just behind the tub. The tub was also circular and also about twelve feet in circumference. Even the walls were constructed of white polished marble and this helped to magnify the glory and intensity of the light in the room. The sinks were also carved from a single piece of brilliant white marble. There was a crystal pitcher of water resting upon the marble sink. I entered and turned to the right to look at the circular window and the tub that was placed directly below it. The angel in attendance to this room was beautiful and smiled at me with acceptance. The angel's beautiful blue eyes also reflected the brilliant light in the room. The angel picked up the crystal pitcher and poured some of the crystal clear water into the tub and stirred the water.

The angel pointed at the tub and I noticed that it was nearly filled with crystal clear water. The water was exuding a wonderful aroma, and it was apparent to me that the tub had been prepared especially for my visit. As the steam rose from the water in the tub, it also emitted heavenly aromas of oils and healing agents that had been stirred into the water by the attendant angel. John 5:4 came into my mind, *"For an angel went down at a certain time into the pool and stirred up the water; then whoever stepped in first, after the stirring of the water, was made well of whatever disease he had."*

For the first time, I realized that the robe I was wearing was dirty and soiled. The angel removed it and left the room. Then I stepped into the tub and began to luxuriate in the warm, healing, waters. The temperature was perfect, and the bath was a welcome and unexpected treat. I soaked in the waters for what seemed like hours. The fragrances were amazing and the water was treated with oils and was silky smooth to the touch. I accidentally splashed some of the water into my mouth and found that it tasted as wonderful as it smelled. The water had an effervescent quality and carried a touch of citrus scent. It was delightfully refreshing in more ways than one.

Through the massive circular window I saw the manicured gardens far below the beautiful stone castle. It occurred to me that this may be the Father's house, but I was not sure. What I was sure of, I was having a wonderful, relaxing, and renewing time soaking in the perfumed waters. I rested my elbows upon the edge of the white tub and allowed my gaze to wander out the window onto the view below. In the distance I could see the river flowing through the land. The thought occurred to me that this was the river of life that proceeded from the throne of God and from the throne of the Lamb (see Rev. 22:1). Yet, as I observed the crystal clear river below, I understood that it was the same healing river that Ezekiel saw flowing from under the door of the temple (see Ezek. 47:1-8).

Over the course of time as I soaked in the water of the tub and contemplated the heavenly landscape below, I also realized that the river

I saw was the same still, peaceful waters of Psalm 23 (see Ps. 23:2). I thought about these things for what seemed like hours as I watched the sunshine reflect playfully off the pure river of the water of life, clear as crystal, proceeding from the throne of God and of the Lamb. I was surprised that my healing bath never cooled. It supernaturally remained at the optimum temperature. As I soaked in this amazing tub in this amazing bathroom, I was being restored, cleansed, and healed. In fact, I would often return to this bathroom to be cleansed and restored before proceeding into the heavenly realms on future visits. After a while I turned over onto my back and rested in the Lord in the sweet smelling healing waters of the tub.

As a matter of fact, I actually fell into a restful sleep in the healing water. I dreamed about an angel handing me a towel and smiling at me with big blue eyes of understanding and compassion. When I woke up, that same angel was standing at the edge of the tub with a large plush towel in hand. I took the towel and smiled at the angel. I rose up from the tub and stepped up out of the water and dried off with the fluffy white towel. The angel then placed a new, immaculate robe upon me. I turned to look out of the circular window again, and a smile filled my face. Pure joy flowed through me at that instant, and the cares of the world were forgotten. In my mind I thought, *It doesn't get any better than this.*

I raised my left arm to look at my new garment. In the sunset, the material shimmered in the light with a supernatural sheen and colors burst from it in all directions. I had never had a robe like this before! I left the bathroom and entered the hallway. I turned to see the angel there wave goodbye and smile at me with tenderness.

## INTO THE LIGHT

I started to walk down the hallway or what I had come to think of as the hall of faith. I walked by many more shields until I came to the opening in the hallway. When I reached it, I found it full of light and glory. In this spot on the right side of the hallway there was an extensive and ornate handrail fashioned of precious metals. It appeared to be constructed of platinum, gold, and silver in a similar fashion to the gate at the entrance to the secret stairs. The handrail had intricate patterns incorporated into the design, and the gold balusters, pickets, and post tops reflected the brilliance of the light of the room above and below.

I was engrossed in observing this railing and did not notice the details of the hall below. I heard a sound echo from the ceiling to my left. Looking up I saw a man suspended upon a platform. In an instant I realized that he was an artist. It was then that I saw the magnificent frescos that adorned the ceiling of this great hall. The paintings that decorated the ceiling were incredible! The room below was massive and the paintings on the ceiling were also enormous.

The artwork in this massive room made that in the Sistine Chapel and Saint Peter's Cathedral appear to be the work of an amateur. The quality of the paintings was unmatched—even by Michelangelo! The brilliance of the color palate and contrasts between the hues was superb! I was overwhelmed by the beauty and grandeur of the designs and the skill with which the frescos had been executed. My eyes were intoxicated by the beauty of the designs and colors.

Suddenly the artist who was working spoke to me, "Why don't you come up here and help me!" He had a brush in his hand as he had just finalized a minute detail of a portrait. He put the tiny detail brush down and turned to look at me, and I realized that he may well have been Michelangelo! I was stunned and stood in silence as I thought about the magnitude of the invitation to help this brilliant artist!

I was wordless and stood silently gazing at the sheer magnitude of this intricate work of art above my head. It must have taken centuries to complete! I relished looking at the murals for a long time. It was astonishing, and I was rendered speechless by the quantity and quality of the art suspended over my head. I was also astonished by the artist's invitation. He turned back to his work, and I turned back to my thoughts. *Perhaps this was the desire of his heart? For Michelangelo this would be paradise!*

# THE GREAT BANQUET HALL

From the corner of my eye I saw a flash of luminescent colors explode below me. I turned to look to my right and below, and that is when I saw Him. Jesus had just picked up a large crystal challis and the light had reflected from the liquid that was within the Lord's cup exploding in every direction. Jesus looked up at me and smiled. In that instant, the glory of God enveloped me, and I began to weep. Within my heart I ached to be with Jesus again.

The Lord was seated at the far end of a very long banquet table; the table was about three hundred feet long and about eight feet wide. The table was dressed out with the finest linens and china. It was surrounded by dozens of beautifully crafted high-back chairs trimmed in gold. There was a smorgasbord of food upon the table and it seemed that Jesus was waiting on someone before He was going to begin His meal.

Jesus looked up and our eyes met for a moment, and I realized that the Lord was waiting for me! I looked behind me and saw a circular stairway leading to the massive hall below. I turned quickly and ran down the hallway as fast as I could manage. On the way down the circular stairway, I noticed that these walls were also lined with the shields of faith from the great cloud of witnesses. I made my way down three or four stories worth of stairs and came to two large, arched wooden doors. They were also hinged in gold and had golden handles in the center of each door. As I scampered across the hallway, an angel stepped forward and opened the door on my behalf. I ran into the great hall where the Lord was seated at the other end of the massive table.

For a moment I was frozen by the glory of God and fell to my knees weeping. It was so overwhelming to be in the presence of Jesus again! Brilliant light and the glory of God filled the place. I found it difficult to move or even think at that instant. After a moment, two angels moved to my side and helped me stand. They smiled at me and gently raised me to my feet. I looked up to see the frescoed ceiling above and realized that the works of art there were even more spectacular than I first understood. I took a moment to absorb the grandeur of the room, realizing that I had been personally invited into the great banquet hall. I was surprised to see that it was totally empty save for Jesus and me. Even the artist was now gone, and only a few attendant angels remained in this place.

The room was massive and the ancient architecture included great vaulting arches and ceilings around the circumference of the expanse of the enormous hall. Far above, ornate windows emitted shafts of brilliant light that illuminated the banquet hall perfectly. Angelic worship filled the air along with the fragrance of Heaven. I looked to my left and saw hundreds of rows of long tables. Each table seemed to be more than three hundred feet long, and they were each dressed out and with fine linens, silverware, and china. The banquet hall was prepared for a great supper (see Rev. 19:9). I glanced at the Lord to see Him still smiling patiently at me, and with a sweeping gesture of His left hand, He called me to Himself.

As I walked toward Jesus, I could once again feel the coolness of the perfectly white marble floor under my bare feet. I could feel my beautiful white robe as it lightly dragged across the white marble floor. I finally entered between two of the elongated tables and began to walk the remaining distance to the Lord who was seated at the head of the table on my right. The closer I came to the Messiah, the more I realized and understood His love and sacrifice for me. Great tears began to well up from within my spirit, and I began to weep as the presence of the Lord intensified as I approached Jesus.

I noted that the table was made ready, the feast had been prepared, and the Messiah sat at the ready. I wondered where the other guests were, but I was so overwhelmed by His presence that I lost that thought quickly.

## AT THE RIGHT HAND OF JESUS

When I came near the end of the table, there were the four angels in attendance to Jesus. These were the same four angels that I had seen previously with the Lord. The table had a fresh-baked loaf of bread in the center of a silver serving tray. There were wine and crystal goblets for each of us. One of the angels pulled out a chair for me to sit down—I was seated at the right hand of Jesus. This was just too much for me! I fell down at the feet of Jesus and began to weep as I received revelation and a small understanding of the magnitude of His sacrifice for me. I simply fell at the feet of Jesus and laid there. I wept. I wept for a long time until finally I felt the hand of the Lord upon my head and I heard the Lord say, "You are welcome here."

I placed my hands upon the Lord's feet and great tears poured from my eyes. This was my first invitation to join the Lord in the great banquet hall. I chose to lie at the feet of Jesus and worship Him. I wept for a very long time as waves of God's love and glory washed over me in rhythm to the angelic worship that filled the great hall. I luxuriated in being at the feet of Jesus. Hours seemed to pass uninterrupted, and I found myself back in my little prayer room at 121 Beech Street. I was unable to move for a long time and continued to weep as the tangible presence of the Lord pinned me to the old shag carpet. I understood that my life had been transformed by this encounter with Christ in the heavenly places.

On subsequent trips to the Father's house, I would often repeat this process. I would walk along the stone pathway and up to the balcony. I would enter through the same two massive and ancient doors and walk down the hall of faith. The white marble bathroom was always open and available for me to cleanse my body and soul. The beautiful angel was always present to hand me the fluffy white towel at the end of my soaking. I was always given a fresh and clean phosphorescent white robe to wear into the presence of Jesus.

Over the course of time, I noticed how the fresco on the ceiling of the great banquet hall was progressing, and saw the artist moving across the upper heights of the great banquet hall as the ceiling was being adorned. I would often lie at the feet of Jesus weeping and luxuriating in this special place.

On my second trip to the great banquet hall, the Lord placed His hand upon my head and told me to "Arise and eat." I did, and after that visit, the Lord and I partook of communion together many times in the great banquet hall. I would often sit with the Lord for communion, and the four angels would attend to our needs and pour the wine for the Lord and me. Jesus and I would often break bread together and enjoy meals side by side in the great banquet hall. We would pray, and the Lord would lead us in taking the Lord's Supper. By the grace of God, I have experienced communion with Jesus in the great banquet hall many times.

After a season of visiting the Lord there, He invited me to visit other places in the realms of Heaven. In the next several chapters I will describe those places and what the Lord's angelic hosts are doing in the heavenly realms today. However, before I get to those testimonies, I need to share with you another recollection of an event that transpired with the Lord in the great banquet hall in February 2002.

CHAPTER 3

# A VISION OF RELIGION

*February 20, 2002, 4:13 AM*

This morning, just a few minutes ago, I was in my prayer closet and the Lord spoke to me. It is not unusual for the Lord to speak to me in this way. I am often allowed to enter into the very presence of Jesus. Sometimes I just bask in His glory not uttering a word. Many times I am summoned into the dining room, or what I have come to call the great banquet hall.

Tonight when I entered the dining room where I usually sit with Jesus, there was a lot of noise. There was a lot of murmuring and chatting. This was surprising to me for two reasons. First, usually only the Lord Jesus and I sit at the banquet table. When I am alone with the Lord, the atmosphere is always very reverent. It is holy, quiet, and very peaceful, so this time I was wondering what was going on. I was very curious; but I love to be with the Lord, so I just relaxed and began to look around the banquet hall.

The hall is massive. The great banquet hall is perhaps two thousand feet long and about fifteen hundred feet wide. Perhaps it is even longer than that; I am not sure of the exact dimensions. In the great hall are beautiful marble floors and very high, vaulted ceilings. The walls are made out of the most ornate carved stone. There are also hundreds of beautiful windows that are perfectly placed above the room. These gorgeous windows are very large. There are amazing frescos that adorn the massive vaulted ceilings overhead. The windows may be about one hundred feet tall and about forty feet wide; they let in the heavenly light from the gardens outside.

## THE LORD'S TABLE

The table that is usually reserved for Jesus and I is very long—about three hundred feet long and eight feet wide. Our table is always covered with spotless white linens. The Lord Jesus always sits at the head of the table, and usually I am seated to His right. We have beautifully crafted high-back chairs trimmed in gold. The table is set with very fine china. The plate that was in front of me was pure white with a ring of purest gold around the edge. There are always three forks, two spoons, and two knives. These utensils are also made of the finest gold. The place setting includes a very fine white linen napkin, but I have never needed to use it.

There is always a big loaf of fresh-baked bread in the center of the table between Jesus and me. The fresh bread is always steaming hot when I arrive, and its aroma is absolutely as good as the taste. I can still smell the lingering aroma of the bread as I write this, it is heavenly! There is always a carafe of gold that contains red wine. There is also always a large crystal clear carafe full of fresh, clear, cool water. I know that the water comes from the fountain of life, or from the living water. I drink freely of both, and there is never a need to refill these two containers. The wine is always in a golden challis, and the water is always in a clear crystal glass similar in shape to a champagne glass. Angels are always in attendance to meet our needs and to refill our cups if needed.

Sometimes I sit at the far end of the Lord's table, and the distance between Jesus and I is about three hundred feet. However, we never need to raise our voices. He speaks very softly, and I can always hear His voice and what He is saying. We do not speak much while we are breaking bread together. I just enjoy being in the Lord's presence. It is very special to be with Jesus in this place, and I feel quite blessed to be invited to dine with Him.

I usually have a big, thick, hot slice of the bread of life. It is delicious all by itself. I often enjoy manna jam smeared all over the bread of life, too. Jars of manna jam are always on the table before Jesus and me. Sometimes there is also sweet meat, which melts in my mouth. What a heavenly feast we enjoy, my Lord and I.

After dinner Jesus usually speaks to me. I am not at liberty to share all of the things that He reveals to me. Sometimes He arises and comes to my end of the table. Other times I go to Him and just lie at His feet; I hear His sayings. Sometimes we go to other rooms in the Father's house. At other times we go out into the other regions of the estate. It is massive and covers eternity. I am writing this because Jesus told me to. Otherwise I would not share these treasures.

## THE NOISY NIGHT

As I shared earlier, this night when I came into the great banquet hall, there was a lot of talking. It was noisy! I was very surprised by this and took a seat at the far end of the beautiful table. Jesus was sitting at His end. There are dozens, even hundreds, of tables within the great banquet hall. Most of the tables had people crammed around them. The people were making a big fuss. Some of the tables did not have a lot of people sitting there, but even those tables were very loud. *The people are being very irreverent,* I thought. I am always very solemn and reverent in the presence of Jesus.

As I sat down, I looked at the other end of the table to see the Lord's reaction to all the noise. He just smiled at me! I looked at all of the noisy dinner guests. I was amazed. There were men, women, and children. It seemed that they were all ignoring Jesus; I wondered what the Lord must be thinking. I assumed that their behavior must surely hurt the Lord's feelings. I looked around again. There were many, many thousands of people in the great banquet hall.

Somehow I knew that they were all waiting on something before they would eat. Many were dressed in fine clothes. It seemed that these finely dressed guests were all seated together in familiar groups at the different and separate tables. Some of the guests wore casual clothing, some wore rags.

I was wearing a white lined robe given to me by the angel that always greets me when I come to the Lord. I first go to the beautiful bathing area where I soak in a large marble tub that is filled with crystal clear water from the river of God. I relax and soak in there until all of the filth comes off me. Then I towel off, and the angel gives me a new, immaculate white linen robe to wear into the presence of Jesus. Sometimes my robe is adorned with a blue sash and sometimes it is a golden or yellow sash.

That is one reason I was so surprised to see the guests dressed so haphazardly. I did not like the way the people were dressed or how they were acting, but Jesus did not seem to mind. I was shocked that they did not seem to care that they were being rude to Jesus by talking so much. I could not hear what they were all saying, but somehow I knew that it was really not important in the eternal scope of things. It was like a buzzing sound. The noise was deafening—and irritating. Jesus seemed to be used to their behavior, and He did not seem to mind their loud talking. The fact that they were ignoring Him did not seem to bother the Lord at all.

I could sense the love and majesty that was emanating from His holy presence. However, it seemed that these people just did not feel the power, love, and glory of the presence of Jesus in their midst. Worse, they almost all seemed to ignore the fact that God Himself was there. They seemed to ignore God all together for the most part. They were more interested in the mundane things that they were speaking and murmuring about. I observed this for quite a while and was hoping that they would soon be quiet so we could eat and enjoy the wonderful feast that Jesus had prepared for us.

I always enjoy eating with Jesus. The very act is as pleasant as the heavenly food itself. We always take our time and savor the wonderful flavors of the fine foods. I always take my time, and eat with as much care as possible. I always try extra hard not to spill any food or wine on the beautiful white linen tablecloth—it is so beautiful and delicate.

After a while of searching the hearts of these unruly guests and trying to figure out why they were behaving in this undignified manner, I noticed Jesus looking at me! The Lord raised His golden challis of wine. I understood that He was giving me a signal to say grace. I always enjoy it so much more when Jesus prays. I took a tiny sip of wine to clear my throat, and I prayed with as much eloquence as I could muster. I prayed the best supplication that I could manage. After all, Jesus is sitting at the same table. What happened next shocked me!

## It Got Ugly

When I finished my prayer, all of the people violently attacked the food! They ripped into the bread of life with bare hands. They spilled the wine and the living water all over the Lord's gorgeous linens. Precious manna jam was smeared all over. I sat there watching the chaos with my mouth hanging open, dumbfounded. The people were fighting over the food, manna jam, and sweet meat—yet there was more than enough for everyone. It got ugly!

I was totally stunned. I watched this carnage for about a half hour. Then I thought, *I wonder what Jesus is doing? I wonder what the Lord is thinking about this crazy, self-absorbed behavior.* I looked at the other end of the table and saw Jesus quietly eating. Jesus instantly noticed that I was looking at Him and He raised His challis to me and smiled at me. He toasted me! Jesus toasted me! No one else in the whole dining room toasts with the Lord, just me. This really surprised me too, but it did not surprise the Lord. I tried to eat my meal, but with all of the distractions, it was very hard. It was really tough.

I did eat, but I did not enjoy the food and being in the very presence of Jesus as I usually do. It seemed that the nicer a person was dressed, the worse their table manners were. None of the thousands in attendance behaved properly. However, there were a few who did look at Jesus, but even these people had horrible manners. Suddenly a big, majestic, golden-inlayed grandfather clock in the far corner of the great banquet hall chimed and gonged. That was it!

## NO THANK YOU, NO GOODBYE

In an instant, all of the people jumped up to leave, spilling more of the precious new wine and living water. Jars of delicious manna jam toppled over onto the marble floor—they spilled their heavenly treasures. The people scattered the precious heavenly food everywhere in their haste to leave. The bread of life was flying through the air and landing upon the usually spotless white marble floor. The linen tablecloths were stained beyond repair with red wine and manna jam. Chunks and crumbs of bread were everywhere—on the tables and under the tables! People spit out mouthfuls of the bread of life in their haste to leave the great banquet hall.

It was sickening to me. They knocked each other down trying to leave the room, rudely leaving the very presence of God. They did not even say thank you to Jesus. I could not help but feel embarrassed and disgusted. I felt ashamed, but I did not understand why I felt that way. When I finally brought myself to look at Jesus, He smiled at me! He was used to this sort of thing. Somehow I had a knowing that this happened all the time.

I was thinking that I would at least offer to clean up the mess. It would take me a long time. Even with the help of quite a few angels it would take several hours to repair what these thoughtless people did in about one hour. I doubted the Lord's beautiful linens could even be salvaged. Just then, as if the Lord understood my thoughts, the entire room was instantly sparkling clean! There was no clue left that there had ever been anyone there. This did not surprise me, but I still felt badly. I felt as if I had some responsibility or connection to this mob of slobs.

## THE CHURCH

Then Jesus motioned me to come to Him at His end of the table. I slowly made my way to Him. I could feel the cool marble under my bare feet as my white linen robe gently dragged on the floor behind me. I still felt embarrassed. When I reached the Lord, Jesus allowed me to climb up in His lap. Jesus put His arms around me. Then the Lord held me close to His breast.

His love and compassion filled me immediately. Waves of His love and grace radiated from Him, filling me with joy unspeakable. The Lord held me for a long time. I always get so filled and touched by the Holy Spirit when Jesus holds me that I don't want to move. I just want to soak in more of His presence, more of His love, more Jesus. I can still feel His presence as I write this now.

Finally after a long silence, the Lord spoke to me saying, "Don't worry My son; it is not your fault. They know not what they do. It is like this every week. What you just saw was the "church." That is the way that they come into My presence. That is the way that they honor Me in most of their temples. Most come to Me to get fed. They grab what they can. I am praying that they really get hungry for Me. I am concerned that the Father may allow famine to overtake many of them. You noticed that some of them behaved better than others. Some of them really love Me. They just forget why they come into My house.

"My son, please tell them to come to worship Me in spirit and in truth. Please tell them that I love them and that I miss them. You know how much I love them. Oh, how I long to spend time with them. If they only realized how short an hour or an hour and a half is here in My Father's house. I long for them to be with Me. Please tell them to worship the Father and Me in spirit and truth. It is important. I do so want to bless them all, but they do not position themselves to receive. They do not stay in My presence long enough to experience the Holy Spirit fully. They miss so many healings, blessings, revelations, and outpourings of the Father's love. Please tell them to wait, be patient. If they just wait on the Lord, I will renew their strength. Oh My precious son, please tell them the time is short.

"Tell them that they have replaced the Father, the Son, and worst of all the Holy Ghost with the traditions of men. They have replaced God with a routine that makes it almost impossible for the power of God to move. Tell them how much I love them and how much I miss them. So many are deceived. So many who think that they are saved are not and they deceive themselves. Tell them, My son, please tell them that religion and a relationship with God are two different things. Religion will not save them. Only My precious blood and a personal relationship with Me can save their souls. I want fellowship with My people. Oh how I long for them to be with Me as much as I long to be with them. I love them so much. Tell them, tell them!"

## THE LORD WEPT

I thought, *Oh Lord, how You must grieve for Your bride.* Just then Jesus began to weep. A deep sense of sadness and loss pervaded the great banquet hall. I could hear the Lord's sobs and cries as He prayed for the Body of Christ—echoing throughout the massive dining hall. Suddenly the massive hall was filled with angels; they were all concerned for Jesus. They were dismayed, too. The angels began to weep uncontrollably. Their tears flowed onto the spotless marble floor and immediately their tears transformed into what appeared to be gold dust. The Lord kept holding me and weeping. He was wailing, and the sound kept echoing. Tears were flowing down Jesus' face and falling upon my cheeks. I began to cry as well. I could feel His pain when His tears touched the skin of my face. Jesus knew this, but He could not bring Himself to stop weeping. I knew that Jesus wanted to stop, but He could not. Jesus held me for a long time until His tears subsided.

Finally, He gently pushed me away from His chest and looked into my eyes. Christ's eyes were burning with passion and love for His chosen people. The Lord raised His right hand and gently wiped our mingled tears from my face. He looked deeply into my eyes again. The Lord has such beautiful eyes, like diamonds, sapphires, and pearls all spinning around.

He looked lovingly into my eyes and said, "Please go back and write it all down. Tell them that I love them. Tell them what you saw and experienced. Tell them how I long for their fellowship, for their love. I died for them so that none would perish. Please tell them that there is not much time. Many of the people you saw here today will lose their earthly lives by Sunday. It may be too late for them, tell them. Tell them how much I love them. Tell the church. Please do not grieve the Holy Spirit."

The Lord stood up, kissed me goodbye, and headed for the massive door that leads to the throne room. I just stood there and watched as He walked away. I did not want to leave His precious presence. Jesus stopped and turned around as if sensing my discomfort. Jesus said, "Don't be afraid My son, you can come back anytime you like. Now go forth and do my bidding. Write it all down. Tell the church the Kingdom of Heaven is at hand."

Then He opened the door to the Father's throne room, and I could hear the worship, "Holy, holy, holy...." A brilliant light flowed into the great banquet hall, and then Jesus shut the door behind him and it was silent for a moment. Then I heard angelic worship gently begin to fill the air around me.

I let out a heavy sigh; and falling on my face, I began to pray for the people I had just seen in this place. From somewhere deep within my spirit, sounds and utterings that I had never known began to erupt from my mouth, and I began to pray in a heavenly prayer language. I interceded in this way for a long time. Sometime later, when I rose up from the marble floor, I found myself back in my little prayer closet. There was a pool of tears on the carpet, and as I got up, I was wiping away tears from my eyes. Then I made my way to the computer that the Lord had given to me and I wrote the words that you have just read.

Please, please don't grieve the Holy Spirit.

As I write these concluding paragraphs today, a decade later, the impact of this experience still causes my heart to skip a beat. Many people do not believe that Jesus, in Heaven, is praying or interceding for His people. But that is one of the roles of the Lord as a royal priest after the order of Melchizedek. Hebrews 7:25 illustrates this role of Christ:

> *Therefore He* [Jesus] *is also able to save to the uttermost those who come to God through Him, since He always lives to make intercession for them.*

In the next chapter, I share another experience in which I witnessed the Lord weeping and interceding for the innocent and the oppressed. This next testimony had a great impact upon my life and was used by the Lord to alter my heart and mindset about God's heart for the poor and the least of these.

# CHAPTER 4

# THE WEEPING ROOM
# A HEAVENLY ENCOUNTER

*Wednesday, February 11, 2004, 2:46 PM*

I was in Enumclaw, Washington, when I had a visitation from an angelic being. The word angel in the Bible is derived from the Greek word *ang'-el-os,* and can mean a messenger; especially an "angel"; by implication, God's angelic beings are messengers. Angels often play a role in making sure that a person receives an important message the Lord wanted them to understand clearly. Angels are heavenly messengers often sent from the very presence of the Lord. This particular angel came to me during a time of prayer.

I do see other angels from time to time. These angelic visitations usually occur in times of ministry, during the release of the healing anointing, or during seasons of extended prayer and fasting. The experience that followed shook me to the very core of my being, and changed the course of King of Glory Ministries International. Perhaps it will change your mindset and worldview, too.

## ANGELIC VISITATION

This particular angelic visitation began innocently enough. I had been waiting upon the Lord for several hours when suddenly the atmosphere in my prayer room became electric. I realized that I was about to have a visitation. I had been calling out to God, asking for the Lord to touch me. I had been positioning myself to enter into the heavenly realms. I had been busy traveling and ministering and had not experienced any recent heavenly visitations. So I had a desire within my spirit to visit with Jesus. There have been many times over the past few years when I have been allowed to experience times of refreshing from the Lord's very presence in the heavenly places.

This type of prayer and ministry is outlined in Ephesians 1:3, *"Blessed be the God and Father of our Lord Jesus Christ, who has blessed us with every spiritual blessing in the heavenly places in Christ."* We can also find the promise of these types of supernatural encounters in Ephesians 2:4-7:

> *But God, who is rich in mercy, because of His great love with which He loved us, even when we were dead in trespasses, made us alive together with Christ (by grace you have been saved), and raised us up together, and made us sit together in the heavenly places in Christ Jesus, that in the ages to come He might show the exceeding riches of His grace in His kindness toward us in Christ Jesus.*

I believe strongly that there are times in our lives when we can actually ascend into the very presence of the Lord and sit together with Christ in the heavenly places. This experience was one such experience.

I was in a posture of waiting or soaking prayer. Really this is meditative prayer, and I was focusing my attention on the Lord. Everything seemed to be normal. Then a series of supernatural events began to transpire in my little house. Here is how it all began.

First I began to sense the tangible glory or presence of the Lord fill the little bedroom I was in. Then the fragrance of frankincense filled the entire house. Immediately I felt a strong, warm hand gently pressing upon my back, and I heard the voice of the Lord Jesus saying "Come up here." I recognized the voice of the Lord, and I certainly "knew" the glory of the Lord that was quickly filling the room I was praying in. The weighty presence of God was literally pressing me into the mattress of the bed. So I simply luxuriated in the tangible presence and the love of God for several minutes. It seemed like an eternity.

Suddenly the warm hand that was pressing into my back moved, and it took a gentle but firm grip of my right hand. Again I heard the voice of the Lord say, "Come up here." When the hand took hold of my right hand, I began to rapidly ascend in the spirit. I have often gone to the heavens, but it was rare that I had an angelic escort. I was reminded of Revelation 4:1:

> *After these things I looked, and behold, a door standing open in heaven. And the first voice which I heard was like a trumpet speaking with me, saying, "Come up here, and I will show you things which must take place after this."*

Certainly I have not often had an angel come to me as I prayed to Jesus. Although it had happened a few times in the past, it still surprised me today. I guess that I was not expecting an angelic visitation during my prayer time. Nevertheless here I was ascending into the heavens, being pulled by the hand of this strong angel. Then I saw a familiar bright light and tunnel of light that I had witnessed before. This phenomenon has occurred from time to time as I ascend into the heavenly realms to visit with the Lord Jesus.

I felt safe. I was going up; but this time I was traveling at a much greater rate of speed than normal. It is possible that my angelic escort was affecting the speed of my ascent today. It seemed as if I was rocketing through the heavens like a shooting star or meteor. I called out to the Lord, asking, "Who is this angel, Lord?"

There have been many times when I have seen the angels in the spirit. But I very rarely speak to them, and they have rarely spoken verbally to me. On the other hand, the Father, Holy Spirit, and Jesus all speak to me. By the grace of God, I am learning to distinguish the difference in each of their voices. They are very clear to me, and I live to be in communion with God. The Lord wants to speak to you, too.

At that moment I heard the voice of the Lord Jesus say, "This is My servant; he is bringing you to Me in a special place. Come up here." That was good enough for me; I began to relax and enjoy the ride. This angelic messenger took me through the familiar tunnel of bright light, and later we went out into the universe. We passed planets and stars, and I just relaxed and took it all in. It was a wonderful experience, and I was never once frightened.

During this time of ascending and sightseeing in the galaxies, I began to look at the angelic being. He was powerful with great wings that spanned nearly fifteen feet. He radiated the glory of the Lord. The angel's body was like that of a weightlifter, and his muscles were well defined. At one point he turned to look at me, he smiled and gave me a knowing wink. I could see his face very clearly. He had long, curly, bright blond hair and blue eyes. A great sense of peace and joy filled me during this time of ascending in the spirit. It seemed like hours that we glided between planets and distant galaxies.

## INTERCESSION FOR THE SAINTS

Suddenly the angelic being and I came to rest; actually we landed in a large room. It was sparsely decorated; not much furniture. The floors were quite plain, made of knotty pine with some cracks in the wood. Because I had seen the most beautiful white marble floors at other times when I have been allowed to sit in heavenly places, these unrefined floors surprised me for a moment. (I now realize the pine planks of the flooring in the room looked just like our cabin in North Carolina, but this experience occurred about five years before we built the new home.)

After the flooring, the next thing I noticed was a great increase of the glory of the Lord. I could smell the overwhelming fragrance of Jesus. The wonderful fragrance of frankincense and myrrh was actually palatable, and it seemed as if I would taste the aroma of the Lord. This powerful angel then took his station in an area of the room. He crossed his arms and placed his back to the wall. The angel appeared to be on guard duty, and I believe I could call him a guardian angel. There were also three other angels stationed at cardinal points around this rustic room. I think they were also guardian angels.

I saw four people in heated intercession. The intercessors were pacing back and forth. Each one engaged in deep travail and prayer and all weeping heavily. I wondered who these prayer warriors were. Perhaps it is possible that they were ordinary people who were engaged in third heaven intercession. Another possibility was that I was witnessing some of the members of the great "cloud of witnesses" (Heb. 12:1). These were people who loved the Lord and had put off every weight of sin that would keep them tied to the earthly realm. Or perhaps they were some of the apostles and saints of old. Somehow, I understood that only a few were allowed to enter into this special place. So I was very surprised to be there.

Immediately the spirit of intercession filled me, and I had a great desire to pray like I had never prayed before in my entire life. Perhaps I was being filled with the spirit of supplication (see Zech. 12:10). I did not know what to pray for, and I did not know what the others in the room were interceding for either. So I just began to groan in the spirit. As I prayed, I examined the room briefly and wondered why I had been brought there. What was I doing there? I remember that I had been in extended prayer and had asked Jesus if I could come upstairs to visit with Him for a while. The Lord had spoken to me saying, "Come up here." Then I had felt the angel's strong, warm hand.

*So what am I doing here?* Romans 8:22 leapt from within my heart, *"For we know that the whole creation groans and labors with birth pangs together until now."* Then I realized that the Lord had brought me here to pray, and I was sure that He wanted to teach me something very important. But what heavenly treasure did Jesus desire to reveal to me in this sequestered and special place?

I dropped to my knees and began to earnestly pray. Beads of sweat began to boil up on my forehead. The sweat began to drip from my nose and puddle on the floor below. I could feel the grain of the knotty pine beneath my knees. I could feel the glory and presence of the Lord Jesus. I could smell the pungent, wonderful fragrance of the Lord Jesus Christ. I could see the four apostles dressed in white robes travailing, weeping, and calling out to God. They paced about the room travailing and laboring in prayer. They were totally unaware of my presence. Perhaps they could not see me; but on the other hand, they were most likely totally engrossed in the Spirit-led intercession in which they were engaged.

I could hear them praying in the Holy Ghost, and I continued to wonder, *Where am I?* It was all very real. I was no longer in the state of Washington. I was no longer praying in a little house, and I was no longer in the cushy little bed. No, I had been translated with the help of the strong angel standing about twenty-five feet to my left. I raised my head to check to see if the angel was still there, and he glanced at me, shooting me a fierce look, and then a slight smile! There was no question—I was in the heavenly places. The Lord had granted my request, allowing me to be with Him this day. However, I had never visited this particular place before when I had been raised up with Christ in the heavenly places. My train of thought was broken when I heard the Lord speak again.

## THE FRAGRANCE OF JESUS

Jesus called to me. Surprisingly, I had not seen Him before—only enjoyed His fragrance. Now, there was an intense glory radiating from Him. The room was filling with a semitransparent, golden fog. I understood that the fog was the manifestation of the glory of the Lord. Jesus was sitting in the middle of a big, rustic, four-poster bed. The bed was heavily made with sturdy, rugged wooden posts. It had a thin, bright white mesh canopy over the top. The Lord had His arms wrapped around Himself, and He was rocking back and forth.

Jesus was weeping as He prayed. When I laid my eyes upon Him, I was overcome with the power and glory of the Lord. I became undone and fell upon my face prostrate onto the pine floor. I could feel the wood grain under my body. Perhaps I was in the spirit because I could actually feel the intense pain and groaning of the Lord's prayers. Tears filled my eyes and rolled down my face and nose to pool below me. I forgot about being in the heavenly realms. I did not care that I was still in prayer myself, and I became lost for a season with Christ in the heavenly places (see Eph. 2:6). I was travailing, weeping, loving, praying, and dying to my needs and personal desires.

I had forgotten why I had wished to come in the first place. Honestly, I had missed this kind of intimate experience with the Lord. It was coming into the heavenly realms and laying at the feet of Jesus that initiated a metamorphosis and total transformation in my life. Frankly, I missed being with Jesus and absorbing His radiance. I missed the intimacy and communion that had started to slip from my life as I had grown busy with ministry and traveling.

Then I began to realize how incredible the scene was unfolding before me. I was in a prayer meeting with Jesus and the great cloud of witnesses. My mind swirled around with the possibilities of these things. I had heard of third heaven intercession, perhaps this was what heavenly intercession was supposed to be like. For a moment doubt entered my mind. At that exact instant, I looked into Jesus' beautiful eyes, and He gave me a warm, gentle smile. Instantly, Romans 8:34 filled my mind, *"Who is he who condemns? It is Christ who died, and furthermore is also risen, who is even at the right hand of God, who also makes intercession for us."*

Then a passage in Hebrews also rolled into my spirit, *"Therefore He is also able to save to the uttermost those who come to God through Him, since He always lives to make intercession for them"* (Heb. 7:25). Suddenly I realized that it was very scriptural for Jesus to be praying and interceding for His children in the realms of Heaven. Of course! Then I began to wonder what exactly Jesus was interceding for and what was He asking the Father?

## THE PRAYERS OF JESUS

The intensity of the Lord's prayers was amazing to witness, and I thought about this during this span of time. Jesus appeared to be praying intensely in the Holy Spirit, too. There was no question about what I was witnessing as I observed the Lord praying. Perhaps that is why the apostles asked the Lord to teach them to how to pray (see Luke 11:1). I wondered if Jesus had been praying in the Holy Spirit when He had withdrawn from the disciples to pray (see Luke 5:16).

Perhaps Jesus had been praying earnestly in the Holy Spirit in the Garden of Gethsemane (see Luke 22:44). That would explain why His disciples did not understand how Jesus prayed. If Jesus was praying in tongues, it would have baffled His disciples, and perhaps that is why they asked Him to teach them to pray. Jesus was certainly filled with the Holy Spirit (see Luke 4:1). And according to Scripture, the evidence of being filled with the Holy Spirit is speaking with other tongues or the gift of tongues (see Acts 2:4, 1 Cor. 12:10). I continued to think about this possibility as these Scriptures flowed freely through my spirit. Did Jesus pray in tongues on earth?

I wondered about this. However, I decided that it was no time for introspection. So I also began to pray in the Holy Spirit according to the model of Jude 20. I did not really know what to pray for or how to pray in agreement with Jesus, so I prayed in the Spirit. It seemed that I was once more lost in time. This often happens in the heavenly realms. Perhaps it is because time as we know it on earth does not exist in Heaven.

It seemed that an eternity of time passed as I interceded in agreement with the great cloud of witnesses and the Lord Jesus Christ in the heavenly realms. Then I heard Jesus calling my name. "Come here," beckoned the Lord. I stood up and walked to the foot of the bed. Christ was still groaning and interceding. He still had His arms tightly wrapped around His sides as He wept intensely. Yet, Jesus looked lovingly and longingly into my eyes. The Lord was imploring me. I thought, *Oh, Lord what could I possibly do for You? Who can be so close to Your heart that You would cry, weep, and intercede in this way?*

Somehow, understanding came to me, and I knew that Jesus invests considerable time here praying. By some means, I knew that Jesus had been here in this place praying for years off and on. What was this magnificent place so full of the glory and love of God? Suddenly, Christ called my name again. I moved over to beside the bed; I was very close to the Lord now. When I looked up, I saw Jesus raise His head from a posture of prayer, and I looked directly into the eyes of the Lord once more. What beautiful eyes the Lord Jesus has; they are the most beautiful and captivating eyes in the universe.

Christ's eyes searched my eyes for a moment, *"The eyes of the LORD run to and fro throughout the whole earth, to show Himself strong on behalf of those whose heart is loyal to Him"* (2 Chron. 16:9). When my eyes met the eyes of God, I felt the indescribable love as well as the deep hurt and heartbreak within His Spirit. Jesus smiled and said "Come." Immediately, I was supernaturally drawn into His eyes. I was sucked into the eyes of Jesus. I began to see what Jesus saw. I could feel what He was feeling. I began to go where He was going. I began to see the children. At that moment I saw what Jesus sees. I saw what was so heavy upon His heart. And in an instant I knew exactly what the Lord Jesus Christ has been interceding for, and weeping over for hundreds of years.

## HIS CHILDREN

One by one I saw the little children. The children who are so dear to the heart of the Father are dying. One by one, they are dying. Every day they are dying, and God is weeping mightily over each and every one of them. They die because of lack of food. They perish because of lack of water. They die because of lack of care and love. They expire because of lack of basic medical care. They die from abuse and war. They die as a result of abortion.

I saw little six-month-old Tully in South America. I saw his father throw him in the garbage dump and leave him for dead because he could not afford to feed another child. I saw the orphans starving to death. I saw children, seven and eight years old, trying to feed their starving younger siblings. I saw mothers trying to nurse their babies but they had no milk in their breasts. I saw the babies dying, and I felt the heart of God breaking for each one. God's children are dying, and not just in Africa.

I saw them in India. I saw them in Mexico. I saw them in Ecuador and Peru. I began to see what appeared to be an unrolling video of thousands of helpless children pass before the eyes of my heart. I saw them in Russia. I saw the babies dying all around the world; and yes, I even saw them in the United States. I saw child after child as they flashed before my mind one by one. As each face would flash before my eyes, I would instantly know everything about the child.

I knew the child's name, his hunger, her pain, and what country and city or village the child lived in. I understood the minutia and every detail of each situation. When I looked through the eyes of Jesus Christ, I had a supernatural revelation of each child's personal needs. It all happened in less than an instant. This scenario repeated itself for what seemed like days. I witnessed thousands upon thousands of at-risk children, widows, and other helpless friends of God pass before my eyes after I had been sucked into the eyes of Christ.

After what seemed an eternity, I found myself once again standing at the side of the bed. The Lord was looking intently and deeply into my eyes. His eyes burned with passion and love. I thought, *Oh, Lord how I have failed You. What can I possibly do?* I was suddenly aware of how selfish my personal lifestyle had become. I was aware of my great sin. I was guilty of the sin of omission. How could I honestly call myself a follower of Christ and do nothing for the ones I had just seen?

Jesus looked with tender compassion and unfathomable love into my eyes. The Lord then placed His right hand upon my left shoulder and said; "Feed My sheep. Care for My children. I will make a way." Instantly these words spilled out of my mouth, "I will do it, Lord!"

# I WAS UNDONE

In a flash I experienced the sensation of my body being vaulted back through the tunnel of light, and I was back in Enumclaw. I was back in the bed that was now soaked with perspiration, and I was undone. The lingering fragrance of frankincense and myrrh still hung in the air. My eyes were burning from the tears I had cried. The weighty glory of the Lord still rested upon me. I lay there for several hours pondering the visitation in my heart. I had really believed that I was righteous, and I had thought that I was on the right track. The scripture from James 1:27 began to burn within my spirit, *"Pure and undefiled religion before God and the Father is this: to visit orphans and widows in their trouble, and to keep oneself unspotted from the world."*

Certainly it is the heart of the Father to preach the gospel to the poor and lost and to feed the poor while caring for the widows and orphans of the world. I was stunned by this experience and began to search the Scriptures to find the Lord's heart in this matter and scriptural confirmation of this experience. I found the words of Jesus concerning how we treat the poor and helpless people in our sphere of influence. Could Jesus really mean what He taught in this parable in Matthew:

> *For I was hungry and you gave Me food; I was thirsty and you gave Me drink; I was a stranger and you took Me in; I was naked and you clothed Me; I was sick and you visited Me; I was in prison and you came to Me.*
>
> *Then the righteous will answer Him, saying, "Lord, when did we see You hungry and feed You, or thirsty and give You drink? When did we see You a stranger and take You in, or naked and clothe You? Or when did we see You sick, or in prison, and come to You"? And the King will answer and say to them, "Assuredly,*

*I say to you, inasmuch as you did it to one of the least of these My brethren, you did it to Me."*

*Then He will also say to those on the left hand, "Depart from Me, you cursed, into the everlasting fire prepared for the devil and his angels: for I was hungry and you gave Me no food; I was thirsty and you gave Me no drink; I was a stranger and you did not take Me in, naked and you did not clothe Me, sick and in prison and you did not visit Me"* (Matthew 25:35-43).

As for me, this was a sobering angelic visitation, and not at all what I had been hoping for when I went into prayer. But what is more important was the message that the Lord released directly into my heart and spirit as He allowed me to see through His very eyes. It was so life-changing that I felt compelled to include it in this book. My prayer is that you will invest some time in introspection and prayer. Jesus Christ is weeping for His children. What have you done for the least of these in your sphere of influence? Perhaps there is a little more that you can do?

After this encounter, my wife, Kathy, and I were at the local Starbucks when suddenly many tiny feathers began to swirl around my head. The anointing and glory hit me powerfully as I was having a hot chocolate! The glory seemed to linger on my body for days after this visitation. There were many times in the weeks that followed when feathers would appear out of nowhere around my body, and this supernatural experience continues to this day! It is as if Holy Spirit is saying, "What you experienced was true and important. I am confirming the experience." I have carried a heightened sense of the angelic realm around me since that day.

In the next chapter, I share another example of a time when I was taken into the heavenly realms by an angelic being. The next testimony may give you a whole new perspective on what it means to be washed by the blood of Jesus.

## Chapter 5

# Washed by the Blood

*Sunday, March 8, 2008, 10:48 AM*

In March 2008, I had just returned from a mission trip to Tanzania. I was grieving for the children at an orphanage that Kathy and I had helped establish in that nation. Through a series of circumstances, the orphanage had begun to struggle and the original pastor we had worked with had slipped into a pattern of sin and deception. We had worked to rectify the situation for several years. However, after returning from this trip, I had a knowing that the children's home was in grave trouble and might soon collapse. In addition to this, I was struggling with many other areas in my walk with the Lord.

I had been in an intense period of personal introspection for nearly a year and a half. I was crying out to the Lord asking Jesus to search my heart and create in me a clean heart. Actually, this process was birthed on October, 3, 2004, in Dudley, England. On that Sunday, I had attended a worship service in the city, and Bobby Connors was speaking. He was preaching and speaking prophetically from Psalm 51. Bobby's message that morning had a profound impact upon me and my walk with the Lord. In fact, from that moment on, I purposed in my heart to pray

Psalm 51 over my life, heart, and spirit. I continue to pray this psalm over my life daily, especially verses 6-11. Little did I know that this precious psalm would lead to a supernatural encounter with the Lord and another heavenly encounter with the Messiah and His angels.

## PSALM 51:1-17

*Have mercy upon me, O God,*
*According to Your lovingkindness;*
*According to the multitude of Your tender mercies,*
*Blot out my transgressions.*
*² Wash me thoroughly from my iniquity,*
*And cleanse me from my sin.*

*³ For I acknowledge my transgressions,*
*And my sin is always before me.*
*⁴ Against You, You only, have I sinned,*
*And done this evil in Your sight—*
*That You may be found just when You speak,*
*And blameless when You judge.*

*⁵ Behold, I was brought forth in iniquity,*
*And in sin my mother conceived me.*
*⁶ Behold, You desire truth in the inward parts,*
*And in the hidden part You will make me to know wisdom.*

*⁷ Purge me with hyssop, and I shall be clean;*
*Wash me, and I shall be whiter than snow.*
*⁸ Make me hear joy and gladness,*
*That the bones You have broken may rejoice.*
*⁹ Hide Your face from my sins,*
*And blot out all my iniquities.*

*¹⁰ Create in me a clean heart, O God,*
*And renew a steadfast spirit within me.*

*<sup>11</sup> Do not cast me away from Your presence,*
*And do not take Your Holy Spirit from me.*

*<sup>12</sup> Restore to me the joy of Your salvation,*
*And uphold me by Your generous Spirit.*
*<sup>13</sup> Then I will teach transgressors Your ways,*
*And sinners shall be converted to You.*

*<sup>14</sup> Deliver me from the guilt of bloodshed, O God,*
*The God of my salvation,*
*And my tongue shall sing aloud of Your righteousness.*
*<sup>15</sup> O Lord, open my lips,*
*And my mouth shall show forth Your praise.*
*<sup>16</sup> For You do not desire sacrifice, or else I would give it;*
*You do not delight in burnt offering.*
*<sup>17</sup> The sacrifices of God are a broken spirit,*
*A broken and a contrite heart—*
*These, O God, You will not despise.*

On Sunday, March 8, 2008, I was attending a worship service at The Gathering Place in Wilkesboro, North Carolina. Deep within my spirit I was crying out to the Lord. My spirit seemed to be broken, and my heart was burdened and remorseful. I was going through a season of the Holy Spirit's work of conviction. He was bringing up to me many kinds of soulish and sinful residue that was still floating around in my soul. I was beginning to struggle with thoughts that maybe the collapse of the children's home was related to my sins and possibly my inability to work through these issues properly. I was wondering if I had sinned in the eyes of the Lord and desperately wanted to be free of this brokenheartedness. Within my spirit I cried out to the Lord asking that He would wash me thoroughly from my iniquity and cleanse me from my sins.

My daughter Miranda was with me that morning, and we were waiting upon the Lord during the worship service. In my heart I was still hurting, and my soul was aching for the orphans in Tanzania along with the other issues I was facing. Suddenly as I closed my eyes during the worship time, I heard the Lord's voice. Then I saw the Lord; He was looking at me in a very loving manner. Jesus extended His hands to me and said, "Come up here. I want to show you something."

Suddenly I felt my spirit rising, and I knew that I was ascending into the realms of Heaven and into the arms of Jesus. I was very surprised because Miranda was right beside me, and I was not really in a "spiritual" state of mind. My heart was aching, and I was hungry for God, but I was not expecting Jesus to minister to me in such a dramatic and supernatural way that morning. Nor was I expecting a heavenly visitation at that moment.

I closed my eyes and felt my body rising up and felt the force of the wind as it flowed across my face. I relaxed as I realized that the Lord was bringing me into His presence. I was both surprised and elated! After a few moments, I sensed that the ascending had ceased, and I opened my eyes to see Jesus smiling at me. I was standing in front of the Lord. All the while the Lord was encompassed by four angels. I knew these angels as I had been in their presence many times before. I was drawn to the beautiful burning eyes of Jesus and His compassionate smile. The Lord said, "Why is your heart so troubled? I want to show you something today, come with Me."

## My Favorite Place in Heaven

It was then I noticed that the Lord was standing in the grassy meadow near the crystal clear waters of Psalm 23. My heart leapt with joy because this is my favorite place to visit in Heaven! Just the realization of where I was brought me great peace as I have invested precious times with Jesus in that place of peace and tranquility. Overhead the sun shone in a beautiful, cloudless sky. The trees that lined the river swayed in rhythm to the worship. I noticed the sounds of harps and other instruments as they wafted through the atmosphere. The music was perfectly accented by angelic singing; and for a moment I was lost in the magnificent sound of angelic worship.

Jesus had started to walk toward the river of life, and I had subconsciously walked beside the Lord as the four angels flanked us on our left and right. As I looked at each one, they smiled and gently welcomed me with a look of reassurance.

Soon we came to the spot that the Lord and I often enjoy. The special place is near an arched wooden bridge that crosses over the still waters of Psalm 23. This beautiful little bridge leads to a warm, shaded meadow full of colorful tiny flowers across the river of life. At the edges of the crystal clear water are all manner of beautiful wild flowers. Dancing around the flowers is always a plethora of multihued butterflies. One of the angels indicated that I should join the Lord who had walked ahead; my gaze had fallen upon the butterflies and I was lost in my thoughts as I watched the butterflies and honey bees dance in harmony with the various flowers swaying in the gentle breeze.

I was again grateful to partake of the wonderful fragrances that wafted along the river of life from the dazzling array of flowers. Their beauty is breathtaking and the fragrance is like nothing on earth. I lingered for just a moment longer in fascination with the spectacular dance that was evolving along the bank of the crystal clear water. Flowers and butterflies were in perfect rhythm with the angelic worship that filled this place. Even the delicate scents and aromas of the flowers were articulated in perfect rhythm to the music. It was fascinating.

I turned to look down at Jesus who had settled onto a plush white rug. The Lord smiled at me and motioned me to join Him with His left hand. The Lord was reclining and leaning upon His right elbow. The four angels stood around us as I moved to lie beside Jesus. I took one final look at the flowers and butterflies and a big smile creased my face as I turned to look at the Lord. Jesus was smiling at me. He had something in His hands. It was fresh, flat bread, and I could smell its tantalizing aroma. Jesus blessed the bread, and as He tore the matzo-type bread into two pieces, handing me the larger half, I noticed the nail scar in His right hand. I was instantly aware of the magnitude of the sacrifice that Jesus made for me. He is the Passover. For a brief moment I started to cry, but the Lord indicated that I should look at Him. Once more I gazed into the beautiful, passionate eyes of Jesus, and instantly I again received revelation and understanding about His love and compassion for me. He smiled. I burst out between a laugh and a sob as I held the unleavened bread. What a price He paid.

## THE LOVE OF THE LORD

I continued to look into the eyes of God and waves of His compassion and His unfathomable love washed over me. The angelic worship continued to fill the air around us like an ethereal soundtrack. The strong, aromatic aromas and the fragrances of the flowers nearby tickled my sense of smell. The four angels continued to encircle us and seemed to be enraptured by what was taking place on our special spot by the river of life. I was almost undone, and in my heart I just wanted to lie at the feet of Jesus as I had done many times in the past.

However, I knew that Jesus wanted to share communion with me. He was still smiling benevolently at me. I gazed into the eyes of my Savior as love poured into my heart. For the tiniest moment I was aware of what Matthew 22:37 really means when Jesus said, *"You shall love the Lord your God with all your heart, with all your soul, and with all your mind."* I don't think that we can humanly love the Lord the way this Scripture directs. However, when we are in His presence, it is not difficult. It will be the only desire of our spirits and souls. In the anointing of Jesus, it is easy to love God with all your heart, with all your soul, and with your entire mind. That morning for a very brief moment of time I did love the Lord as commanded.

My thoughts were interrupted when one of the angels reached between the Lord and me. He took a large golden pitcher and filled two crystal goblets that were on the small serving platter between us. As the angel handed me one of the goblets, I saw that it was full of fine and majestic wine. The bouquet of the wine was fabulous; it seemed that I could taste it from the aroma alone. My senses were on overload. The angel then gave Jesus the second crystal goblet. I was mesmerized by the events that I was experiencing. The bright sun continued to shine and sparkled off the goblets in a rainbow of supernatural colors. Angelic worship continued to envelop us as the butterflies and flowers danced in perfect rhythm to the Lord. For a moment I was lost in my thoughts once more.

The voice of Jesus interrupted my contemplation. The Messiah was blessing the bread. Then He said, "Take, eat; this is My body." Then I took the matzo bread from the Lord's hand and ate it. I was expecting it to be sort of bland, but to my surprise it was delicious. The flavor that exploded in my mouth was like cinnamon, honey, and almonds. The bread seemed to melt in my mouth and a wonderful sensation of wholeness and cleansing spread from my mouth throughout my entire being. I closed my eyes and luxuriated in the sensation as the angelic worship filled my ears, and the fragrances of this special place inundated my sense of smell.

Every fiber of my being was crying out, "Thank You, Jesus!" The Lord spoke again, "Take and drink, for this is My blood of the new covenant, which is shed for the remission of sins." I looked into Jesus' eyes as He held up the crystal clear goblet filled with the fragrant red liquid. An enormous smile spread across the Lord's beaming face. He slightly tilted the crystal goblet in my direction. Rainbows of colors danced off the crystal as the sun seemed to ignite the goblet and the contents within it. Jesus drank the contents of the goblet, then placed the chalice on the tray between us.

As I placed the crystal goblet to my lips, the anointing of the Holy Spirit rushed through my entire being. I lifted the goblet and slowly drank every drop. The taste and bouquet of the liquid was unlike anything I had ever tasted on earth. When I had finished the fragrant red liquid in the crystal goblet, I slowly set my glass down on the silver serving tray between us. Heavenly light danced from both of the crystal goblets to the silver serving tray, which reflected another rainbow of supernatural colors around us. The silver serving tray was ornately engraved with delicate filigree and ornamental designs that were obviously of heavenly origin.

Somehow I felt different, and I was aware that a great weight had been lifted from my shoulders. I was lost in my thoughts again. In my spirit I was praising and thanking the Lord for His finished work on the cross. My train of thought was broken when Jesus rose up.

Jesus looked back at me over His right shoulder and motioned with His head that I should follow Him. The Lord walked purposely toward the crystal clear waters of Psalm 23. I stood up and walked a few paces behind the Lord, and the four angels walked along with me. When Jesus reached the river, He stepped right into the clear water. This surprised me. In the past I had witnessed Jesus walk right across the top of the calm, clear water, and I had even walked on the river of God myself when Jesus had invited me to join Him. Walking on water gives a real sense of liberty.

## TODAY, I BAPTIZE YOU

By now Jesus was waist deep and He was motioning me to come to Him in the clear water. When I stepped into the water I was accompanied by the four angels. The water was refreshing and warm. My bare feet stirred up the sandy bottom of the place where we were standing. I looked down and saw gold and silver dust and flakes swirling in the gentle current. As they drifted by, the flakes reflected the heavenly sunlight from above. As I was marveling at this sight, the Lord reached out and placed both hands upon my shoulders.

Suddenly I was aware that the four angels had flanked me and that Jesus was about to baptize me! I placed my right hand over my nose and held my wrist with my left hand. Jesus said, "Today, my friend, I baptize you in the name of the Father, the Son, and the Holy Ghost." Jesus took my head in His hands and leaned over as He submerged me into the river of God. As I fell backward, I was not fearful but rather elated, and I saw Jesus smiling at me as I rose out of the crystal clear waters. I was also surprised to see that the four angels had caught me and helped the Lord as He lifted me out of the waters.

Jesus then took His hands and began to rub the hair of my head. I felt a warm sensation and it seemed that something was dripping off my head. I glanced down at the crystal clear waters and noticed that blood was dropping from my hair into the water. I was startled and reached up to feel my head. When I did, I felt the Lord's hands and my right index finger accidentally pierced the open wound of Jesus' left hand. I was shocked and thought that I may have caused Jesus pain.

## WASHED WITH HIS BLOOD

I looked quickly at the Lord, and He was still smiling at me. He stepped back slightly and held His hands out in front of Him. I was startled to see blood seeping from the Messiah's hands. I must have looked a little faint. With a soothing smile, Jesus reassured me that it was okay. He then stepped closer to me and began to rub His bleeding hands over my head. Jesus rubbed His blood upon my face. He washed my ears, eyes, nose, and whole face with His blood. The Lord continued to gently wash me with His blood. The Lord applied His blood over me the same way a loving father would wash a newborn baby. He gently caressed my hands, fingers, chin, and so on. Jesus washed me thoroughly with His precious blood.

Jesus covered every part of my body with His blood. At one point as I had my eyes closed, it seemed to me that the Lord reached into my chest and took my heart into His hands. With both hands, He began to wash my heart with His blood and gently massaged my heart. When He finished, He motioned to the four angels and they helped Jesus as He placed me in the water a second time. When I came up out of the water, the robe I was wearing seemed to glow—and there was no trace of the precious blood that Jesus had scrubbed my entire body with.

I glanced at the waters of the river of life and they were perfectly clean and clear. There was no trace of the blood of the Lamb that had washed me clean. I saw only the flakes of gold as they reflected the morning sunshine in this magnificent place. This greatly surprised me, and I realized that the blood of Jesus is the most powerful and supernatural substance in the universe. I looked down again to see Jesus reach down into the water with His right hand and pluck something from the sandy river bottom. When Jesus opened His hand to show me what He had picked up, there was a large perfectly faceted diamond resting in the center of the palm of His hand.

When the Lord held the diamond up higher, the sunlight hit it and began to diffuse hundreds of rainbows of brilliant supernatural colors in all directions around us. The colors began to bounce off the surface of the still waters of Psalm 23. I watched for a moment as the rainbows of colors danced from the Lord's hand. The four angels standing around us swooned slightly and I noticed that the rainbows of colors were also dancing off the angel's immaculate phosphorescent white robes. The angels smiled and we all watched as this supernatural light show danced off the water around us.

I looked at the magnificent gem that appeared to be about the size of a golf ball. It had hundreds of facets. Truly this diamond had been fashioned and cut by an extraordinary artist; and I understood that it was of great value. To my astonishment, the Lord reached out His hand and gave me this amazing heavenly treasure. I held it up in the sun for a moment to watch the rainbows of light dance once more, and then I placed it in a small leather pouch that was attached to the golden sash around my waist. What a precious gift. I was stunned by what had just transpired.

We all stepped out onto the grass beside the river of God. It seemed that I was instantly dry and the love of God supernaturally abounded within my heart. Jesus and the four angels were all smiling at me for a moment. I was lost in my thoughts wondering what I had just experienced. Jesus stepped forward and placed His right hand upon my left shoulder. He looked lovingly into my eyes and said, "Never doubt the power of My blood to cleanse you and make you whole. My blood is the most powerful substance in the universe. When My blood is applied, it can never be removed. You are marked and cleansed. Now go and remember that you are washed in My blood."

Instantly I was back in my body with my hands raised in worship of the Lord. The worship team was still playing and streams of tears were rolling down from my cheeks. The lyrics the worship team was singing rang in my ears, "What can wash away my sins, nothing but the blood of Jesus. What can make me whole again, nothing but the blood of Jesus." Tears of joy were freely streaming down my face, and I had forgotten where I was in the natural realm. Suddenly I felt a tug on my shirt. I looked to my left to see Miranda looking up at me with her big brown eyes. "Are you all right, Daddy"? I sat down beside her and looked into her eyes and said, "Yes, honey, Daddy is all right because the blood of Jesus is everything that we need."

In the next testimony, I take you back in time to 2002 and share several sequential visitations into the heavenly realms. In these experiences, we will travel to many places in Heaven including the Father's library, the reading room. We will also visit some of the vaults of Heaven to discover hidden mysteries of Christ's Kingdom. Later we will travel to other places in Heaven including Psalm 23 and the river of revelation, the Lord's manicured gardens, the fountain of living water, and finally the Father's vineyard. Along the way we will meet many magnificent angelic beings who populate the heavenly realms.

CHAPTER 6

# THE LIBRARY PART 1
# HEAVENLY PLACES

*March 8, 2002, 5:48 PM*

As the evening sun began to wash across the old porch at 121 Beech Street, it bathed the weathered, peeling paint with a golden amber glow. The color reminded me of the beautiful hues I had seen on my excursions into the heavenly realms. I sighed as I put the aged metal key into the brass, timeworn lock. It had been a long and weary day toiling on an old home. I was tired and covered in paint chips and caulk. In my heart I longed to be with the Lord so I could feel His presence and Christ's unimaginable love once more. As I turned the key and entered the living room, the glory of God plummeted upon me, and I immediately fell to my knees and began to weep.

The Holy Spirit was waiting there to welcome me home! It appeared that He had missed me as well. I turned to my right and pushed the old, black front door closed. Then I fell upon the floor and wept for a long time as waves of the love and presence of the Lord washed over me. The presence of God felt golden, much like the color of the evening sunset that was washing over the old porch in the colors of Heaven. I lay there luxuriating in the anointing and presence of the precious Holy Spirit. This was a little kiss from the Lord.

After about an hour, I scrambled to my knees and thanked the Lord for visiting me again. I took off my dirty work clothes and filled the old-fashioned bathtub with warm water. As I stood at the sink scrubbing the caulk off of my hands and from underneath my fingernails, I glanced into the mirror at my face. There were trails where my tears had poured through the dirt of the day, and I began to laugh. But then once more I began to cry as the realization of the love and deliverance that the Lord had given to me was tangible and so unquestionably real to me today. I smiled and stepped into the tub.

I soaked in the bathtub and prayed as I allowed the warm water to remove the dirt and cares of the world from me. I longed to be with the Lord; and in my spirit, a heart's prayer was birthed from somewhere deep within my being. "Lord I wish I could just wait in Your presence all the time. I wish that I did not have to go out into the world and toil. I would like to pray and enjoy the presence of the Holy Spirit all the time."

When I finished cleaning up, I stepped into the tiny bedroom and got dressed. As I finished, the Lord said, "Kevin, look." When I heard this, the eyes of my heart were opened and I saw a vision (see Eph. 1:17-21). In the vision I saw an ancient scale held in the right hand of Father God.

## A METAMORPHOSIS

The scale was totally unbalanced with the right side down and the left side high. Then I watched in amazement as the scale methodically began to supernaturally move until the trays were perfectly balanced. When they reached this point, the Lord said, "I will begin to establish you in the ministry that I have called you to. From this day on you will see your secular job decrease and your ministry increase." As the Lord was saying this, understanding percolated up from within my spirit and I understood that the Lord was starting a metamorphosis in my life that would take me from my secular job into full-time ministry. This process would unfold just like the scale moved in increments until it reached 50 percent. As these thoughts flittered through my mind, the vision continued to unfold and I saw the scale move again—40 percent, 30 percent, 20 percent, 10 percent—until finally the scale was at 100 percent on the opposite side. I knew that this movement of the scale symbolized transformation in my life; from full-time secular work and toil into the fullness and joy of serving the Lord from abundance of His Kingdom each and every day.

My thoughts were interrupted by the voice of Jesus saying, "Come up here." I turned and leaped into my prayer room—the little bathroom. I lay down on the carpet and positioned myself to hear the Lord. The little room was still steamy from my bath. Once more I heard the Lord say, "Come up here." Immediately I could feel my body ascend and my spirit also began to soar as I understood that I was being allowed to join Jesus, to be seated in the heavenly realms with Him once again. I went through the familiar process of moving upward through the earth's atmosphere. Once again I could see the little house below as I bolted higher. I could see the same sunset that had been washing the old rickety porch at 121 Beech Street now setting farther west. The colors were spectacular. I continued to ascend until I came to rest in the heavenly places.

I landed once again on the stone walkway, and once again there were two angels who welcomed me and served to cushion my landing. They helped me stand and get my "sea legs" so to speak. They smiled at me and welcomed me back to the holy place. I could smell the fragrances of Heaven, and off to my right were the beautiful gardens I had seen many times before. Once more I thought, *I need to explore those gardens soon.* I looked up to my left to see the great stone mansion sitting majestically upon the hill, and this verse came into my mind:

> *For we know that if our earthly house, this tent, is destroyed, we have a building from God, a house not made with hands, eternal in the heavens* (2 Corinthians 5:1).

I was standing before the house of God in the heavens! I began to jog toward the pathway that leads up to the secret stairs. I was yearning to see Jesus again. After I had jogged about a hundred yards, my thoughts were interrupted by the loud roar of a lion. I thought, *That's funny, I have never seen any lions here before,* then dismissed the thought as I opened the beautiful metallic gate at the entrance to the secret stairs.

I dashed up the stairway as fast as my legs would carry me. I did not stop at the seven flat rest areas. I usually linger on those and look out at the heavenly gardens and the crystal clear waters of the river meandering majestically below. But today there was urgency in my spirit to get to Jesus. I reached the large oval balcony in front of the two large wooden doors leading into the Father's house. For just a moment, I walked over to the edge and rested my hands on the smooth, cool, grey stones and treated myself to a quick glance at the gorgeous scenery below.

When I turned to go into the mansion, I saw a familiar angel who was holding open the large wooden door on the left side. He smiled at me and welcomed me to enter. As my eyes locked with the beautiful blue eyes of this massive angel, I thought, *Man he has a great job! I would rather be a doorkeeper in the house of God—because one day in His courts are better than a thousand days on earth* (see Ps. 84:10). As I passed by the angel to enter into the hallway of faith, I noticed how strong and tall he was. He was perhaps eight or nine feet tall, and was arrayed in an immaculate white robe, which glistened in the golden rays of the evening sunset. Colors shimmered from his robe, and, for a moment, I watched them in fascination as I passed into the hallway. Once again the angel smiled at me with a welcoming grin and allowed me to pass unhindered into the Father's house.

## NECESSARY CLEANSING

Once inside, I noticed that my robe was soiled and I was reminded that I needed to head to the bathroom. As I approached, the attendant angel was there to escort me in. Once again the tub had been prepared and the scented waters had steam escaping from them. The attendant angel poured some of the water from the crystal pitcher and stirred the waters in the tub. Without hesitation I disrobed and slipped into the tub and began to soak in the perfumed, cleansing waters.

I seemed to fall into a peaceful sleep after a few minutes and awoke to the sound of angelic worship filling the air of the bathroom. Remembering where I was, I turned and looked out the beautiful circular window and gazed upon the beauty of the gardens below. Once more I saw the sunset glisten off the crystal clear waters of the river below. I observed this majestic and regal landscape for a long time as I luxuriated in the fragrant waters of Heaven. I soaked in the warm, swirling, sweet-scented waters allowing them to thoroughly cleanse me. Somehow I understood and knew that it was important for me to be cleansed in this way before I visited the Lord today.

Later I stepped from the tub seemingly refreshed, cleansed, and prepared to enter into the presence of the Lord. The angel handed me a fluffy white towel, and I dried off and stepped up to the sink to look at myself in the mirror there. A new robe was given to me and I stepped out into the hallway of faith and walked quickly to the opening that overlooks the banquet hall below.

When I reached the open area, I quickly glanced down into the great banquet hall. All of the massive and exquisitely dressed-out tables were still in place. Looking toward my favorite table, I saw the Lord Jesus seated at the head of the table. My heart leapt, and the Lord called out to me, "Come here." Jesus was motioning for me to come with His right hand. There were four angels standing in a semicircle around the Lord. The evening sunshine was filtering into the banquet hall from the massive and ornate windows above. A beam of bright sunshine reflected from the crystal carafe that was on the table in front of Jesus. The sunshine caused colors to cascade from the crystal in all directions in a rainbow of hues. I looked at the sparkling shades of supernatural colors for an instant before dashing to the circular, grey stone hallway leading down into the great banquet hall.

Hurrying past the shields of faith in the hallway, I noticed many shields with small golden name tags underneath. I found my way into the great banquet hall and once again ran across the white marble floor in the direction of Jesus. I was still about five hundred yards away, but I could see the smile on the Lord's face. He was glad to see me. The marble felt cool and clean on the soles of my bare feet.

When I reached the Lord, I fell at His side and waves of His love washed over me in billows. Tears began to pour from my eyes, and I knelt at the feet of Jesus. My tears fell upon His feet, and I held on to the Lord's feet, sobbing for a long time.

After a while, the Lord placed His right hand upon my head and said, "Come here." As I stood up and looked directly into the eyes of Jesus, it seemed that my very being was melting. I became lost in the Lord's benevolent gaze, until I noticed one of the angels motion me to sit in the chair that he had pulled out for me. So I sat at the Lord's right hand and smiled at Jesus. His tender eyes seemed to smile, too. The angel handed me a fresh white towel to wipe my face and hands. I used water from another crystal basin that a second angel was holding for me and wiped my face and hands thoroughly.

One of the other angels poured a fragrant red wine from the crystal carafe by my white, gold-trimmed dinner plate. The Lord took some matzo bread in His hands, and looking up, He blessed it. Then He broke off a piece and handed it to me and we partook of the Lord's Supper together. When we finished, I sat with the Lord for a long time and He spoke to me about many things. I am not at liberty to write more about those conversations here.

## "I WANT TO SHOW YOU SOMETHING"

A long time passed and the Lord smiled at me graciously and said, "Come, I want to show you something today." As we stood up from the table, several angels approached and immediately cleared the utensils and other items from our places. Jesus and I began to walk to the far northwest corner of the great banquet hall. I was surprised because we usually walked to the southeast corner and went out the doorway to the other balcony that leads down to a different stone pathway. That route also leads down to another section of the river of life and Psalm 23. I was hoping that we would return there today, but I was also curious as to where the Lord was leading me.

Jesus walked by dozens of the long banquet tables. As we passed them, I wondered how many people the Lord was expecting for dinner. Surely there were to be many thousands as there were hundreds of tables and each one was elaborately adorned and dressed out for a scrumptious meal. No food had been served yet, but the silverware and the wine glasses were all in place. It seemed to me that each table would seat at least three or four hundred people with ease. It appeared to me that the meal would be taking place soon. As I thought about this, I looked up to see the Lord Jesus smiling broadly at me, and He said, "Blessed are those who are called to the wedding supper." That made a lot of sense to me. I did not know anything about the wedding supper of the Lamb. Although, I had heard the phrase a couple of times before, it was new to me. I purposed in my heart to find out more about the wedding supper of the Lamb after I returned home.

In a couple of moments, the Lord walked up to a large section of the stone wall and stopped. He said to me, "Do you see?" I looked around, and I looked up and down the massive wall. It was perhaps several hundred feet long and almost as many tall. I did not see anything and shrugged my shoulders. Jesus pointed with His right hand and said, "Here," and touched a small stone lightly. A rumbling sound filled my ears and I jumped back for a second. Instantly a hidden entrance opened in the massive wall. I would have never seen it without the help of Jesus. The stone door slid smoothly to the side. Light appeared to be coming from the opening and the four angels preceded us into the long corridor behind the hidden door.

Jesus indicated that I should take the lead and the Lord followed closely behind me. I was amazed that this hallway was there; I turned and asked the Lord, "Where are we going?" Jesus said, "Today I am going to show you some hidden mysteries." This statement made my mind spin. I was not aware that there were hidden and secret things in the Lord's Kingdom. Imagine; secrets in Heaven. So I found the Lord's statement fascinating.

As if He knew the secrets of my heart, the Lord then said, "There is nothing secret that will not be revealed, nor is there anything hidden that will not be made known to my friends." I was flabbergasted, and at that point became truly excited to reach the end of the hallway and our mysterious destination. By now there was a muted but bright light illuminating the end of the hallway.

CHAPTER 7

# THE READING ROOM

*March 8, 2002*

The angels preceded us down the secret hallway and took up stations at the cardinal points of the room that we entered. When I stepped through the door I was amazed to find myself in a beautifully appointed sitting room. Jesus crossed over and sat down in a very old and ornate high-back Victorian chair. The fabric was red and white in design and the chair had elaborate golden trim and vintage looking feet and arms. The chair looked very comfortable and well-worn. The Lord crossed His legs and relaxed. There was a very large and beautiful marble fireplace upon which the two sitting chairs were focused. The Lord motioned me to take the chair opposite His; as I moved to it, one of the angels placed a very beautiful sitting jacket upon my shoulders. It fit perfectly and was quite comfortable. The material was an extremely soft red velvet and it was a pleasure to have it touch my skin. I sat down with the Lord Jesus, and He smiled at me again.

It occurred to me that there are many hidden entrances in the Kingdom of God. Many times these are only visible to us when the Lord opens our eyes to see them. These concealed entrances often lead to secrets and other hidden mysteries in Christ's Kingdom. It is the Father's heart to give us the Kingdom and all of the secrets and hidden mysteries that are buried within. That is one of the things that we will do in Heaven. We will invest eternity learning more about our awesome God. We will learn to seek out the hidden and mysterious things to be found in Heaven.

As the Lord and I spoke to one another, I began to examine my surroundings. It appeared that we had come to a reading room. On the table to the Lord's right were several books stacked up; it appeared that He had been reading several of these at one time. Each tome was marked with a beautiful golden embroidered bookmark. In the reading room it was silent save for the sound of Jesus and me as we spoke to one another. There were also the subtle sounds of a brisk fire burning in the fireplace. The light and heat from the fire was soothing, and gave a supernatural ambience to the reading room. It was quite cozy and nice to relax with Jesus here. Somehow I understood that this was a very special place to the Lord and that He often retreated here alone to read and to study.

I glanced over my shoulder to see two other angels who were obviously assigned to this place. I am not sure, but perhaps these angels were on guard here, assigned to protect this room. As I was staring at one of the two guardian angels, our eyes locked, and I was surprised by the fierceness in his countenance. His eyes were piercing and seemed to burn with the anointing of the Holy Spirit. This angelic being was robed in a brilliant white robe and on his feet wore leather sandals with golden trim. Around his waist were emblements of war, and a large sword was sheathed in a very ornate scabbard upon his side. He did not smile.

I had become lost in my examination of the reading room; when I turned to look at Jesus, I saw that He was reading one of the books stacked beside His chair. The light from the fireplace released the perfect amount of glorious light to read in this room. I thought that perhaps I should read too. I rose from my chair and inspected the room again. For the first time, I noticed that it was shaped in a perfect circle. The reading room was massive—at least one hundred feet round in my estimation. Perhaps that is why I had not noticed its shape before now. The walls were very high, and I noticed the smells of myrrh, leather, and old books mingling together in the air.

Looking above the fireplace, I saw a masterpiece of art decorating that space. The painting looked to be a Michelangelo or perhaps a Rembrandt. I was mesmerized by the painting and stepped closer to look at it in detail. As I neared, the light from the fireplace reflected off my robe and supernaturally highlighted the painting above causing the colors to dance. It was exquisitely executed, and the color palette suggested one of the Dutch masters. However, I was certain that this work of art was much older. It was framed in a beautiful frame and upon closer inspection I was sure that the frame was actually pure gold with silver inlay. The frame was cool to the touch. I glanced at Jesus, and He smiled at me. I was somewhat surprised that He had such a beautiful painting in the reading room. Although, I am not sure why. Jesus obviously has wonderful taste in art work and in literature. The painting depicted the glory of God hovering in a portal of sorts, in what appeared to be the Garden of Eden. The painting was fantastic and a perfectly rendered work of art.

## His Books

Suddenly thoughts popped into my mind. *I am in the Lord's reading room! What kind of books would the Lord Jesus have here?* I was sure that His books were certainly fantastic. You see, I love to read. I have always loved investing time reading a good book. Perhaps that is one reason that I like to write from time to time. Turning, I saw the attendant angel looking at me with fierceness and a gaze which with I was not too comfortable. It appeared that He was guarding the Lord's personal library! The angel raised his powerful right hand and pointed to the wall on the opposite side of the room. I saw wide gold wristbands on his arm; and for the first time, he seemed to smile ever so slightly. I understood that I could look at the books on that side of the reading room.

I paced quickly over to the other side taking in my surroundings as I walked passed the four familiar angels who were at the cardinal points of the reading room. The room's walls were 100 percent covered with shelves of books. Save for the lone painting, fireplace, doors, and the windows that were high above. At the apex of the shelves were thousands of scrolls stored and categorized with precision. I knew that these were some the most ancient writings in the library. There must have been tens of thousands of books in this one room. At that moment it dawned on me that these books and scrolls were the property of the Lord Jesus.

This insight caused me to smile, and with the smile came the revelation that He had read them all! I walked over and turned in a slow circle taking in all of the reading materials in the room. It was amazing! It was then that I noticed there were large vault-type doors at various points in the room. These doors looked just like the doors of bank vaults on the earth, but they were much larger. It was obviously to me that whatever was concealed behind them was of great value to the Lord. At other points around the room were large elaborately trimmed entryways leading into other hallways.

I walked over to the section where the angel indicated that I could look at the books. It was then that I noticed the ladders that were mounted on wheels that I could use to get to the books that were categorized and stored upon the higher shelves. Each ladder was crafted into an ingenious system that allowed them to move freely and there were about a dozen that served this area of the reading room. The ladder nearest me was fashioned from fine mahogany wood and had platinum and gold trim. Testing it with my right hand, it moved effortlessly with the slightest touch of a finger.

## FATHER'S LIBRARY

I chose to look at the books that I was able to reach while standing on the floor. I was not sure of how to maneuver the ladders. Later I learned that it was the attendant angel's duty to fetch books from the upper shelves. I pulled two books from the lower shelves and glanced at them. They were heavy, and one was written in a language that I did not recognize. I held one book up to my nose and smelled it. It had an aroma of old leather and myrrh. My attention was broken when Jesus called my name. The Lord pointed to a hallway about sixty feet from my position. One of the guardian angels moved next to me and began to escort me to the hallway that Jesus had indicated.

At that moment, I realized that I was in the Father's library! Of course—the reading room was just one small nook of the library. I came to the hallway, and the second guardian angel joined the first angel and me. Each one stood at my side and escorted me into another branch of the Father's library. I remember thinking, *Who would have written all of these books?* There were millions of books in this one branch of the library alone. The walls were lined with books top to bottom, and it appeared that each wall was nearly sixty feet tall. Again the top sections of the shelves were filled with what appeared to be ancient scrolls. The room seemed to go on for eternity.

The hallway was about forty or fifty feet wide and there were beautiful stained glass windows that allowed a perfect amount of light to enter into the area. Each of these magnificent stained glass creations was about forty feet tall, and there were velvet-cushioned seating areas in each window well. Each one was designed perfectly into its unique position and they varied in the amount and hues that filtered through them. These stained glass windows were works of art in themselves depicting various scenarios from the Scriptures. Many I recognized, but others I did not. I took some time to look at the design that depicted Abraham and Isaac on the mountain from Genesis 22. I knew this design was a precious prophetic portrait of Father God as Jehovah Jireh.

## THE SOLITARY BOOK

I walked haphazardly down the hallway. Then I remembered that the Lord Jesus had pointed to this hallway, so there was surely a book in this area that He wanted me to see. I searched for a long time, perhaps three or four hours. I investigated a multitude of books. There was an amazing variety of books on a great multitude of subjects. Each section contained books that pertained to a specific individual. Suddenly I saw a section of the library's wall that had one lone book on the shelf. The solitary and lonely book appeared to glow slightly. It seemed there was an anointing coming from that book, and I was drawn to it. I walked over to it with the two guarding angels escorting me and bent down slightly to look at the title of the book. When I read the title I was shocked. I stood up and noticed that one of the angels was smiling at me. Pointing at the book, he said, "It is permitted for you to read the book." The title was written in beautiful golden letters in English: *Miranda T. Basconi.* Miranda is the name of my daughter.

I picked up the book and ran back the length of the hallway into the reading room where Jesus was absorbed in a large, ancient book. I burst into the room with the two guarding angels at my side. I moved quickly to the chair and sat down with a plop, holding the book in my hands. Jesus looked up from His reading, smiled at me, and said, "This is why we have come to this place today." Then I noticed that my hands were shaking. Jesus smiled at me and reached out His hand to take the book. With both hands, I reached out and handed the book to the Lord. Leaning forward slightly, He opened it and began to read the first few pages of the book. A smile crossed the Lord's face, and He looked up from the pages and handed the book back to me.

I took the open book from the Lord's hand and turned it around. Looking at the title page, I saw an intricately detailed logo and writing in a fine filigree lettering. I opened the book further and began to read. The text contained my daughter's thoughts and dreams. There were pictures of some of the events in her life. I saw a picture of the day that she had fallen onto a rose bush and cut her lip. In the picture, the Lord Jesus was standing beside her, and it was obvious that He had caught and protected her from additional harm. I became engrossed reading the book of my daughter Miranda's life. I read up to the time that she was about six years of age and then I could not bring myself to read anymore. I closed the book and tears filled my eyes. Sitting back in the chair, I realized that the Lord had my daughter in the palm of His mighty right hand. Emotions from a deep and hidden place began to boil up from within me, and it seemed that I was being healed of deep and hidden wounds.

## IN THE PALM OF HIS HAND

A long time passed as I prayed for Miranda in the presence of the Lord. Great peace and contentment was released to me as the knowledge that the Lord was guarding her and He would protect and keep her always. When I opened my eyes, the Lord was looking intently at me and then He opened His arms inviting me to come to Him. I placed the book on the small table beside me and rushed into the arms of Jesus. For some reason, great tears began to flow freely from my eyes, and I cried in the arms of the Lord. I wept for what seemed like hours as the Lord gently held me in His arms of love. I could sense the compassion and all-encompassing love of Christ for me and also for my daughter. After a long time, I pulled away from the Lord and He spoke into my heart regarding Miranda.

A great peace of mind filled my spirit and I embraced the Lord Jesus again. I wept once more, and after a time I must have drifted off into a peaceful sleep. When I awoke, I was back in my little prayer closet. I lay there for a long time recounting the events of the experience that I had just walked out in the heavenly realms. I rose up and noted the event in a small journal and made a few notes on the old PC in the kitchen. By now it was past 6 AM, I had been in the heavenly realms for over twelve hours. It is possible that I had actually been in Heaven even longer. It seems there is no real time line when you visit Heaven—time may even cease to exist as we know it. This particular visit to the reading room gave me a lot of revelation and encouragement.

## OUR BOOKS OF LIFE

Every person upon the earth has a book of life that is carefully stored in the library of Heaven. Our books are being written each and every day of our lives. There is an infinite number of endings that our life stories can have. The Lord is carefully cataloging our lives and He has each of our books of life stored in the Father's library. One of the many duties of God's angelic beings upon the earth and within the realms of heaven is to record, write, and scribe the books of life for each person who is conceived upon the planet Earth.

Scripture mentions or refers to these books as the books of remembrance in Malachi 3:16:

> *Then those who feared the Lord spoke to one another, and the Lord listened and heard them; so a **book of remembrance** was written before Him for those who fear the Lord and who meditate on His name.*

From time to time the Father calls for an individual's book to be brought to Him and opened. At that time the Lord decrees judgments on that person's behalf. The Father speaks from His throne of mercy, judgment, and grace, and His righteous decrees affect our lives and present circumstances in supernatural ways upon the earth. I believe that this dynamic was what helped to transform my life and circumstances during this season. Your life and circumstances can also be supernaturally transformed as the Lord decrees upon your behalf from His throne of mercy and grace. You should carefully consider this fact.

God's angels write these books. These scribe angels are anointed to write, and they often manifest and visit us when we discuss and meditate upon the things of Christ and the Lord's Kingdom. Scribe angels are assigned to help individuals write things upon the earth. Many times these kinds of creative angels work in symphony and harmony with the Holy Spirit and help an individual accomplish the task of writing a manuscript or other project that is ordained of the Lord. His angels heed the word of the Lord and go forth to perform it (see Ps. 103:20). I wrote about this kind of angelic activity in my books, *Dancing with Angels 1 & 2.*

After this experience, I began a radical search of my old King James Bible, looking for confirmation in the Scriptures concerning the books that I had seen in the Father's library. I discovered this passage in Revelation 20:12 when Jesus revealed it to me later:

> *And I saw the dead, small and great, standing before God, and* **books were opened. And another book was opened, which is the Book of Life.** *And the dead were judged according to their works, by the things which were written in the books.*

I pray that your name is found written in the Lord's Book of Life. God has made that easy for us. All that you need to do is pray to receive Jesus Christ as Savior, and your name will be recorded and cataloged in the heavenly library. If you want to receive Jesus Christ as your Lord and Savior, you can right now pray the Prayer of Salvation that is found at the end of this book.

After those initial experiences when I was allowed to be seated with Christ in the heavenly places in the Father's library, I went through a season when the Lord often took me into the reading room. During those times, I was given the privilege to read a lot in Heaven. This transformed my mindset and helped me to see the Scripture in a different light. It was also during those times that I was given the opportunity to explore the library in the Father's house.

I had many wonderful experiences in that place, and I want to share a few that I believe will be inspiring to you and may give you hope and insight into your heavenly home. In fact, I returned to the Father's library within just a few hours. On that visit I encountered some of the most fascinating angelic creatures that I had ever seen in the heavenly realms, and I share that testimony with you in the next chapter.

CHAPTER 8

# THE LIBRARY PART 2
## SECRET PLACES

*March 9, 2002, 11:38 AM*

The very next day I was once again taken up into the heavenly realms in a time of prayer. In fact, I had elected to stay home from my job and seek the Lord. I had determined to search the Scriptures for confirmation concerning my experiences in the reading room and in the Father's library. I had invested the morning scanning and scrutinizing the Scriptures. I was seeking some similar incidents in my trusty old King James Bible. This was the same Bible that was blasted off of my chest in Newfoundland by the fireball from Heaven. Honestly, I had not found anything that really helped me up to that point—although Ezekiel had some interesting supernatural experiences, and he did see some scrolls. In fact, Ezekiel ate a scroll (see Ezek. 1). But there were no examples that I could find of houses in Heaven in the Old Testament, which I had searched diligently that entire morning.

So I decided to seek the Lord in prayer once again. I positioned myself in the little prayer closet and began to pour out my heart to the Lord. It short order I found myself being catapulted upward and I realized that I was Heaven bound once more. Once again I smiled and understood that I was going to be with the Lord soon. I landed on the stone pathway. My angelic friends were there to greet me and cushion my landing. I repeated the process of leaping up the secret stairs to enter into the Father's house. I took little time to gaze upon the beautiful gardens below and the crystal clear river that flowed in the distance. However, I did imbibe the fragrances of the flowers and plants that grow in abundance there. Once again the angelic doorkeeper allowed me to enter, and I rushed into the bathroom to be cleansed and receive a new robe from the angelic attendant there.

I walked quickly down the hallway of faith and downward through the circular stairway that leads to the great banquet hall. I burst into the great banquet hall to see the artist working on the ceiling. He waved at me, and I also greeted him. As I walked toward Jesus, I wondered who the artist was. The Lord was waiting at the end of our preordained table with the four angelic beings that always accompanied me in the heavenly realms with Christ. Once more I was overcome as I entered into the presence of Jesus as the power and love of the Messiah washed over me in waves and billows. When I reached the Lord, I fell upon my face at the Lord's feet to worship the Son of God. I stayed in that position for a long time and immediately forgot the reason that I wanted to visit Jesus that day.

After some time, the Lord placed His hand upon my head and I rose to sit with Jesus at the banquet table. The angels present prepared grapes and sweet bread for us to eat, and I enjoyed a meal with the Lord. I was mesmerized by His tenderhearted smile and all-consuming love once more. The sweet bread we shared together was amazing! I can only compare it to cinnamon rolls on earth, but the sweet bread was made of manna and was swirled with fruit that I have never tasted on earth.

This meal gave me a burst of supernatural energy and a new understanding of angel's food. I sat with the Lord for a long time, and we enjoyed a feast in the great banquet hall. Taking a meal with the Lord is always one of my favorite experiences in Heaven. I would later that day visit the Father's vineyard where Jesus gave me a tour of the landscape there. We walked through the vineyard together with my four angelic hosts, and I witnessed angelic farmers harvesting the sweet and juicy grapes of the heavenly realms. I saw other angels harvesting wheat and other grains in the Father's fields, too. There is more about Father's vineyard in Chapter 15.

After a time, I told the Lord about my morning, and how I had searched the Scriptures for confirmation concerning our last meeting in the reading room. I asked Jesus about the Father's library and the millions of books and scrolls that I had seen carefully stored there. The Lord gave me three confirmations, telling me to read John 14, Malachi 3, and also Revelation 20. I had not thought to look in the New Testament in my zealous search. Nor had I plowed through the Old Testament to the book of Malachi either! I made a mental note not to repeat that mistake.

## THE SPECIAL BOOK

When we had finished our meal and the Lord had answered all of my questions, He stood motioning me to follow Him. That is a great thing to do, follow Jesus. The Lord returned to the hidden hallway at the northwest corner of the great banquet hall and activated the apparatus that triggered the entrance to the hidden hallway. The unseen door supernaturally slid silently open to the left. Once more we walked the length of the hallway accompanied by our four attendant angelic friends and helpers.

When we entered the round reading room, the Lord signaled one of the two guardian angels stationed there to bring Him a book from the upper section of the shelves. Jesus spoke to the angel in a language that I did not understand. Then Jesus walked over to His high-back Victorian chair with the red and white upholstery design and sat down. He relaxed in front of the fireplace. I stood by for a moment and watched the angelic being. The guardian angel walked over to the other side of the circular room and moved one of the ladders to the section where the book Jesus had requested was stored. I was surprised that the angel just did not fly up to the top, but then I noticed that the angels stationed in the reading room did not have wings. Although angels without wings can certainly fly!

The powerful angel climbed the ladder with dexterity and ease. He reached the book and placed it under his right arm. The angel was about thirty-five feet up in the air when he retrieved the book. Then he slid down the ladder in one fluid motion reaching the bottom in about one second. That surprised me as well. Apparently this angel had repeated this process thousands of times over the centuries. The angel walked purposely over to the Lord and handed Him the book. As the angel turned, he smiled at me ever so slightly. Perhaps he was becoming more comfortable with my presence in the Father's library? I sat down and watched as Jesus opened the book to a specific page and began to read. I looked up at the painting over the fireplace and studied it for several minutes. I became lost in my thoughts until I heard the Lord clear His throat, which drew my attention back to Him.

## THE MASSIVE VAULT DOOR

Jesus smiled at me again and said, "Look down there." Then the Lord pointed with His right index finger to one of the doors in the reading room. I could see the scar that is still upon His hand. When He pointed, one of the guardian angels let out a little sigh of surprise. I stood up and began to move toward the large door that the Lord had indicated. Both guardian angels fell in step beside me and escorted me to the place where the Lord pointed. When we reached the door, I was surprised at its massive size. It was perhaps twenty feet tall and at least fourteen feet wide. It was enormous, and I could not imagine how much the vault door weighed.

One of the strong angels stepped forward and initiated a series of turns and manipulations on wheels and knobs that protruded from the face of the vault door. This supernatural vault door seemed to be fashioned of stainless steel, or perhaps platinum. I could see the mirror image of the fire in the reading room flickering in the reflection of the highly polished metal. There was the sound of a hermetic seal being broken and then sweet-smelling air rushed out by my head causing my hair to ruffle in the wind created as the massive door was unsealed.

The angel who had manipulated the metal wheels and knobs then opened the door, swinging it to the right. This allowed me to see into the vault clearly for the first time. Bright light was pouring into the reading room from the vault and this surprised me for some reason. In fact, the light made it very difficult to see very far into the vault. The angel then took up a position on the right side of the vault door, and his companion took up the other position of the left side of the vault door. They assumed the position and stature of guardian angels—the two angels were standing at the ready.

I looked back over my shoulder at the Lord to see Jesus motion me to enter the vault. I was about to enter a fascinating room in the Father's library—and the experience changed my life!

# CHAPTER 9

# THE LIBRARY PART 3
# THE VAULT OF MANTLES

*March 9, 2002*

I took a step forward, and then I could see clearly the sheer size of the room that the door had hidden. I also saw two mighty angels move from the center of the room and come quickly to the door to meet me. These angels were bigger than the two guardian angels at the entrance to the vault and they emanated the glory and power of God. It was clear to me that these angelic beings were the overseers of this section of the Father's library and that from time to time they were called to take some of the objects that were stored here to the Father in the throne room. Perhaps that is why these two angelic beings carried so much of the Lord's glory and tangible presence. For a moment I was blinded by the light of these two angelic beings' countenance as the golden glory of God radiated from their faces and garments. It was very difficult to see them clearly.

When the first angel reached me, he spoke to me saying, "Kevin, you are welcome in this place." I had frozen in my tracks and stopped at the threshold of the vault when I saw the two new angelic beings rapidly approaching me. I was gripped with the fear of the Lord. I was surprised that the angel spoke to me and called me by name. This helped ease my trepidation.

When I stepped into the vault, I looked over my surroundings. The angel who had spoken to me said, "You are free to look at all of the contents of this place and you may have whatever it is that pleases you." The angel's voice oscillated and undulated as he spoke. I was shocked to see that these angels had many wings and they seemed to be floating about. The wings of these two angelic beings hovered around them in all directions at once, sort of like a gyroscope. There were wings or wheels within wings or wheels.

## EXOTIC ANGELIC HOSTS

The angel's wings moved supernaturally fast and were blurry when I tried to focus on them. Perhaps I could compare the movement of the wings to that of a hummingbird's wings, but I believe that the wings of these angelic beings moved about much quicker—if it were possible. The other thing that was mesmerizing about the movement of the wings of this pair of angels was the explosion of colors released from the fluttering of their numerous wings. It also seemed that each angel had several faces, but all I could make out were eyes, because their heads moved so fast within the spinning circle of wings or wheels. There seemed to be no instant when their eyes were not perfectly focused upon me. I found this a little unnerving, but sought to look at them in the eye nonetheless. Still, this was nearly impossible because of the constant motion of the three sets of wings and the cascades of light and colors that were constantly reflected from the numerous pairs of wings.

In fact, there seemed to be a colorful halo that encircled each of these angels as they moved in rhythm and in step with me as I explored the vault. The angel's faces also moved and pivoted on their necks in a supernatural fashion. This pair of supernatural beings emanated the very glory of God, and to be in their presence was awe-inspiring. After a few minutes of walking around in this vault with these two colorful and exotic angelic hosts, I turned my attention from my angelic compatriots to the contents of the vault. It was then that I become conscious of the fact that this was certainly a very special place.

This was also an important part of the Father's library. Perhaps that is why the door was vaulted and guardian angels were posted outside and also accompanying me on my exploration of this special place. The book shelves were similar to the ones that contained the millions of books in the other sections of the library that I had visited up to now. The ladders were also similar that enabled someone to reach what was stored on the higher shelves. I was unsure what was stored in the vault, and the thought entered my mind, *I wonder what is kept here.* The first angelic being that had greeted me flitted up next to my head and said, "These are the mantles of the saints." And with that the angel zipped around in a circular motion in front of me and seemed to gaze into my very spirit for an instant before whizzing off at a ninety-degree angle. This revelation of the saints' mantles caused my heart to race, and I began to look at the contents of the shelves more closely.

## THE MANTLES

There were a multitude of boxes carefully arranged and wrapped to perfection. These boxes were placed in perfect order, although I do not think that they were placed in alphabetical order or any type of chronological order that we would recognize as humans. The boxes were stored in an angelic numerical system that is beyond my ability to comprehend or describe to you. But I can tell you that these two angelic beings were well able to find any item stored in their care in an instant, with precision and lightning speed!

As I walked through the vault looking at the contents, the two angelic beings zoomed around me like gigantic, angry bumble bees. However, they were not angry, just excited that a human being was actually walking in their presence. Somehow I understood that I was not the first person to be in this special place; however, it may have been a long time since they had received a visitor. Perhaps that was why the two angelic beings were so excited.

I began taking boxes from the shelves and examining them. Each box was carefully wrapped and sealed. They also had beautiful name tags attached to them. I saw boxes that contained the mantles of saints of old, and I saw mantles of people who had lived in more recent times such as Smith Wigglesworth, Maria Woodworth Etter, Kathryn Kuhlman, and William Seymour.

I picked up the box that contained William Seymour's mantle. It was very ordinary and plain compared with many of the other boxes. As I held Seymour's mantle in my hands, I received a new revelation: in the near future, there would be a new outpouring of the Holy Spirit like the world experienced at Azusa Street. It would be a centennial revival of sorts and would sweep further and wider than the first one was able to reach back on April 14, 1906.

Humility will be the key to sustaining these approaching moves of the Holy Spirit. These revivals will be notable for the level of creative miracles and the number of healings and miracles that will transpire in them. Signs and wonders like this will lead to millions of salvations, and people of every nation will come to receive Jesus as Savior. This will also include the Jewish people who are truly the apple of God's eye.

This understanding brought a smile to my face, and I placed the mantle of William Seymour back into its respected place with reverence. One of the angelic hosts buzzed my head again and I followed it into the vault further still. There were thousands upon thousands of boxes containing the mantles of men and women who loved the Lord and served God in their lives. I saw the mantle of Padre Pio, and it emanated the peace of God. Pio understood and realized how to actually enter into the rest of the Lord. In Heaven, Pio's understanding of this was accredited to him as one of the greatest achievements of his earthly life. I saw the mantle of ordinary believers that were stored and cared for with as much reverence and attention as the mantles of the giants of the faith.

This section of the Father's library was immense, and I was relishing my time there because of the very tangible intensity of the anointing of the Holy Spirit and the glory of God. I must admit I was also enjoying observing my two angelic guides—it was amazing watching them maneuver around on their gyroscopic wings. Supernatural halos of color exploded from their wings as they performed acrobatic maneuvers in the air of the vault. When these two angels flew through the sunbeams in this section of the library, a kaleidoscope of supernatural colors exploded in all directions from their wings. This ignited a spectacular light show though the vault and the spectrum of colors released in this way were spectacular to behold.

On more than one occasion I stopped and rested for quite a while in one of the window well seats and watched the two angelic beings' aerial antics. I am not sure, but these two angelic beings may have been cherubim like the ones described in Ezekiel 10. Then I realized that I had been in the vault for a very long time, and at that point the same angelic being that had first spoke to me flew up and said again, "You are welcome in this place. You can choose any mantle that you wish." I must have spent hours wandering around in the vault of mantles.

## THE DECISION

When the angel told me, "You are welcome in this place. You can choose any mantle that you wish," I received an epiphany and revelation of my visit to this vault in Heaven. Jesus wanted to give me something tangible and valuable. If I could have any mantle that was stored with such care in this place, that meant that the Lord Jesus had arranged for me to have that opportunity. I determined in my heart to choose a mantle that would be pleasing to Jesus. I prayed and asked the Holy Spirit to give me wisdom. I was walking in the vault of mantles because the Lord had allowed me to enter, and it was clear to me that the Lord Jesus had a specific purpose for this excursion. I also realized, from my previous trips into Heaven, that I would return to the earth with revelation about Christ and His Kingdom. This sort of knowledge and revelation just sort of attaches itself to you when you enter into the presence of Jesus. And a similar dynamic was unfolding at that instant when the cherubim spoke to me.

At that instant, an understanding and new revelation was birthed within my spirit. When you stand in the glory of God revelation knowledge comes easily! These mantles are stored in the heavenly realms for a purpose. You see, when the Lord knits a person together in his or her mother's womb, He has a preordained destiny for that one in His Kingdom. God places mantles upon individuals even before our birth. Yet, many of us fail to achieve all that God ordained for us to accomplish upon the earth. The reasons for this vary. God gives us freedom of choice, and we can choose to live our lives however we desire. Sometimes we miss our calling or fall into sin, thus halting our divine destinies. At other times we understand the call of God upon our lives, but we choose to live selfishly for ourselves and to pursue our own carnal desires.

Many talented artists and musicians were actually given creative mantles or anointing by God. However, they chose to use the Lord's talents and anointing for their own purposes. Even men like computer-technology entrepreneur Bill Gates were endued by the Lord with the talent and intellect they have used to grow rich and famous. I believe that Bill Gates carries a God-given "Joseph's anointing or mantle," and he is operating in it to a degree. The 1960s singing group The Beatles is another example of this dynamic. They were given a gift of worship by God. John, Paul, George, and Ringo had a mantle or anointing from Heaven given to them by God. At times they all touched upon the anointing of the Holy Spirit and even many of their secular songs ring true as love songs written to Father God if you listen to them with that in mind. George Harrison sought God and began to function in the anointing to worship for a period. But they all chose to use their mantle or gifting apart from the calling of the One True God.

God gives each of us a choice.

That is why the Son of God prayed, *"Father, if it is Your will, take this cup away from Me; nevertheless not My will, but Yours, be done"* (Luke 22:42). Even Jesus had a choice. Jesus chose to follow the Father's perfect will. However, sometimes we humans do not follow our heavenly Father's perfect will for our lives. Therefore there are mantles that are never fully used. Romans 11:29 teaches us that *"the gifts and the calling of God are irrevocable."* This also applies to the anointing of the Holy Spirit that the Lord places upon us as individuals at the moment of inception. The anointings of grace that God bestows to an individual will never evaporate, and they are never lost. God stores in the heavenly realms the unused anointings and mantles of every person who has ever lived—and these mantles and anointings are available to you and me today as we seek to serve the Lord.

Some people can "pick up" the mantle of a person who had lost a mantle or who refused to fully operate in their God-given mantle in life. Katherine Kuhlman stated that the anointing and mantle that she ministered in was given to her after others had refused to pay the cost to carry the anointing of the Holy Spirit or the mantle of the Holy Spirit that was upon her. Nothing is wasted in the Kingdom of Heaven, and that includes anointings and mantles. God retrieves these and tenderly cares, catalogues, and stores them for future use. Again, this is yet another duty of God's angelic hosts.

## MY CHOICE

This understanding renewed my vigor, and I walked farther into the vault. By now I could no longer see the main entrance; I had passed other side entrances into this place. In this section of the vault of mantles, many of the mantles seemed to be relegated to people who had lived in the first century. Suddenly I saw one mantle that drew my attention. It appeared to glow and it was wrapped in a beautiful, golden box with ornate, blood-red filigree trim. Attached to the box was a golden name tag: *The Mantle of Stephen*. I reached for the box as one of the angelic beings once again buzzed around my ears. When I touched the box with my hands, the power of the Holy Spirit coursed through me. Immediately, the two angelic beings moved near and hovered around me in sweeping circles. They seemed to be genuinely excited. I held the box that contained the mantle of Stephen in my hands for a moment, and I thought about this man, Stephen.

Stephen was a man full of the Holy Spirit. He was full of faith and power, and Stephen did great wonders and signs among the people of his day. Stephen recreated Christ in his sphere of influence and demonstrated the Kingdom of God with miracles, signs, and wonders. Stephen saw the Heaven open, and he gazed into Heaven and saw the glory of God; he saw Jesus standing at the right hand of God in the heavens. Stephen spoke and preached with the power and the authority of the Holy Spirit. He had supernatural insight into the Torah, and we have one of the greatest sermons of the early church recorded as preached by Stephen in the book of Acts. Even as Stephen preached, the glory of God emanated from his face, and the people reported that he had the face of an angel. Stephen was a man after God's own heart. Even when Stephen's countrymen were stoning him to death, he pardoned them and prayed they would be forgiven.

Yes, the mantle of Stephen was the one that my spirit and heart longed for. Turning toward the first angelic being that had spoken to me, I said, "I will have this one." Both angels immediately turned and moved in the direction of the entrance to the vault. I followed them. From time to time one would buzz back to me as if encouraging me to move faster toward the Lord's presence. I carried the ornate box that contained the mantel of Stephen. It took a long and determined walk to reach the reading room with the box in hand. I had not realized that I had trekked so far into the vault of mantles. The two angelic overseers of the vault stopped at the entrance to the reading room. They seemed to salute me as I left the vault, and I noticed that one wrote quickly in a large ledger of sorts that was on a gold-trimmed, fancy wooden podium nearby. I watched the two cherubim's move in a quick 180-degree turn and shower me with one last cascade of light and glory as they pivoted and returned to their assigned stations.

I stepped through the opening of the vault with the box containing the mantle of Stephen. The large angel on the right side of the door was waiting for me, and I handed the box to him. He handed the box to the other angel. Then he turned back to the vault door and closed it, which stopped the brilliant light from shining into the reading room. He manipulated the dials, knobs, and wheels on the vault, and I once again heard the sound of a hermetic seal being activated. Then the guardian angel took the box that contained the mantle back from the second angel and together we walked to where the Lord Jesus was seated. I had been absorbed in observing how the angel had closed and sealed the vault so I had not noticed that Jesus was now looking at us excitedly. When we reached the Lord, the angel held the box at an angle so that the Lord could read the inscription easily.

Jesus said, "You have chosen well," and smiled in a great and mighty way that I had rarely seen. The Lord then made a circular motion with His right hand and the two angels moved closer to me. One carefully opened the lid of the box. As the lid came off, it released a wonderful fragrance of frankincense and roses. One of the angels gently took the garment from the box and held it up between his thumbs and forefingers for the Lord to see. As the robe or mantle unfurled, it reflected the light of the fire and from the window overhead. The mantle of Stephen emitted a supernatural glow and a burst of phosphorescent colors escaped from the white translucent material. I was astonished at the beauty of the garment. It was both extremely light weight and substantial simultaneously, which was quite remarkable actually.

## THE MANTEL OF STEPHEN

The mantle of Stephen was beautiful; it shimmered with color and life. It radiated with the anointing of the Holy Spirit. Jesus stood and motioned me to stand before the two angels and before Him. The two angels carefully placed the garment upon my shoulders and a bolt of power raced through my spirit as Jesus placed both His hands upon my shoulders and looked deeply into my eyes. He smiled again and said a second time, "You have chosen well. May this mantle serve you fully. Freely you have received and freely you may give, as the Holy Spirit leads." I knew that the Lord was talking about the ministry of healing. He was speaking of creative miracles, the gift of special or unusual miracles. The Lord was referring to impartation of spiritual gifts according to the scriptural dynamic of Romans 1:11.

The garment was very smooth and soft. It was made of a similar material that the robes that are worn in Heaven are created from. However, the mantle of Stephen was obviously made of a much more valuable and rare substance. Perhaps faith was an element of the mantle's fabric? It was silky smooth to the touch, and it seemed to radiate colors when the light hit it. At times it appeared to be red, and at other times it appeared to be purple or blue. It shifted color, yet every color was magnificent and extraordinarily beautiful. I was amazed to be wearing such an incredibly beautiful and rare mantle.

I was also aware that anyone could wear this same mantle. It is available to you, too. The mantle was made in a loose fitting way. On earth we would call it a "one size fits all" garment. To minister in the anointing or mantle of Stephen you do not need to become a martyr. God can use an individual in spectacular miracles without sacrificing them. However, at times it is possible for a person to pour out their lives as a drink offering unto the Lord in this way.

As the Lord's hands rested upon my shoulders, waves of power and glory pulsed through me and I began to feel weak in the knees. Jesus allowed His hands to rest upon me for a moment longer, and then He indicated that I could sit down. I sat in the high-back Victorian chair that had been provided for me in the reading room. The intensity of the power and presence of the Lord was overwhelming me at that moment. So I relaxed, resting and luxuriating in the glory of God for a long time. I pondered these events in my heart while I waited in the Lord's presence. A smile of gratitude spread blissfully across my face, and I said, "Thank You, Lord Jesus."

Eventually I drifted off into a restful nap. All of the walking in the vault of mantles with the two cherubim escorts had made me a little tired. I awoke to the sound of my voice saying, "Thank You, Lord Jesus," and I reached down to feel the silky smoothness of the new mantle on my right arm. The garment felt alive and amazingly smooth, and I opened my eyes to see it again. When I looked at my right arm again, I was surprised to find that I was now back in my little prayer closet. It was now very dark outside. I checked the clock and it was nearly 4 AM. I lay there in the prayer closet and meditated upon what I had just seen and heard.

Later that morning, I ripped into the Scriptures of my old King James Bible to read John 14, Malachi 3, and Revelation 20. I was just turning to the book of Revelation as the sun began to rise. I thought to myself how prophetic it was that the sun was rising as I was receiving revelation from God's Word. I decided to stay home from my job again and wait upon the Lord for another day.

I continued to meditate upon those Scriptures over the next several weeks and it seemed that the more I studied the Word of God, the more intense and more frequent my trips to Heaven became. In fact, I became so focused on the Lord and the Kingdom of Heaven that I began to lock myself in my little house and pray and fast for days at a time. Many times when I would position myself and seek the Lord in this way I would be taken up into the heavenly places to be seated with Christ Jesus. Colossians 3:1-3 became a lifestyle for me:

*If then you were raised with Christ, seek those things which are above, where Christ is, sitting at the right hand of God. Set your mind on things above, not on things on the earth. For you died, and your life is hidden with Christ in God.*

The Kingdom became more real to me than my current, arduous life upon the earth. I simply began to exist so I could be raised up and made to sit in the heavenly places in Christ Jesus (see Eph. 2:6). In fact, later that very evening after I had studied the Word of God in my old King James Bible and rested up a bit, I was able to visit the Father's library once again. Jesus allowed me to visit a new part of the library—and this room contained something that truly astonished me. It was even more amazing than the two cherubim. What I discovered in that heavenly place helped me to believe God to release creative miracles as I pray for the sick. I outline that excursion into the heavenly places in the next chapter.

CHAPTER 10

# THE LIBRARY PART 4
# SPARE BODY PARTS

*March 9, 2002*

I pressed into the Word of God all morning. The Lord had given me three scriptural confirmations on my last excursion into the heavenly realm. The Bible tells us that everything should be confirmed by the mouth of two or three witnesses (see Matt. 18:16, 2 Cor. 13:1), so I had asked the Lord for confirmation of the things that I had been seeing and experiencing in my visits to Heaven. It was a great pleasure to stay home and press into reading God's word and to invest time in the presence of the Holy Spirit as I prayed. Truly, I would rather do that than scrape lead-based paint from the old house I was working on. Besides that, it was too cold to paint and there was a chance of rain. So I locked the front door, unplugged the phone, and devoted the day to the Lord.

Since I had been traveling into Heaven the past few days, the presence and the anointing of the Holy Spirit increased and was more tangible in the little house at 121 Beech Street. In fact, I was sure that angels were hanging around my little tabernacle. So I purposed in my heart to entertain them. I had read in the book of Hebrews that a person could entertain angels without being aware of it. So in my mind, since angels had entertained me literally in the heavenly realms, I felt obligated to return the favor. After all, the angels had met me when I arrived. They had helped give me a tour of the region, and angels had even served me fabulous food while I dined with Jesus in Heaven. So it seemed natural to me to make a point of blessing the Lord's angels here in my little home on earth!

You know what? They responded! I had many encounters with angels in the little house over the next two years. It was apparent to me that I had cracked or ripped open the heavens over the little house, which provided free access into the heavens there (see Isa. 64:1). I could go up, the Holy Spirit and God's angels could come down. Of course the most important place where the Lord created an open heaven in this season was within my heart. I relaxed upon the bed in the little bedroom and studied the Scriptures that Jesus had given me as confirmation.

I had read John 14 before. But I never saw the fact that Jesus has actually gone ahead of me into Heaven to prepare a place or abode for me. I found that amazing! When I read verses 1-3, I began to weep because I understood that this one passage alone perfectly defined my previous visit to the great stone castle in the heavenly realm. Jesus said:

> ***In My Father's house are many mansions;*** *if it were not so, I would have told you. I go to prepare a place for you. And if I go and prepare a place for you, I will come again and receive you to Myself; that where I am, there you may be also. And where I go you know, and the way you know* (John 14:2-4).

I could not believe my eyes when I first read this. Houses in Heaven! And what was more, they are built by God for us. The Lord was giving us an invitation to be where He is. And it is certain that Jesus is now in Heaven, and we can be with Him there, too (see John 3:3, Eph. 4:8-9).

I had never thought about the fact that a person did not need to die to be with Jesus in Heaven. I had never heard that preached in church. In the book of Malachi I saw where the Bible speaks about how God will open the windows of Heaven. I thought, *That is exactly what I am experiencing; God has opened the heavens over me and He is pouring out blessings upon me in this little place.* In my heart I never wanted to leave the little disheveled house. It was Heaven on earth to me. The verses in Malachi also referred to a book of remembrance that was written. That made me think, and I remembered how I had seen angels writing in what appeared to be books. Of course, God has angels who write! Apostle John said that he saw so many million angels in Heaven that it was impossible for him to comprehend their number or to count them.

In Revelation 5:11, John testified that:

> *I looked, and I heard the voice of many angels around the throne, the living creatures, and the elders; and the number of them was ten thousand times ten thousand, and thousands of thousands.*

It made perfect sense to me now. All of those millions of books that I had seen in the Father's library were scripturally confirmed. Then I saw what Jesus had told me to read in Revelation 20 about books in Heaven, *"I saw the dead, small and great, standing before God, and books were opened.* John said in verse 12, *"And another book was opened, which is the Book of Life. And the dead were judged according to their works, by the things which were written in the books."* If God will open every individual's book of life upon the earth, there must surely be millions upon millions of books in Heaven.

Scientific studies suggest that as many as 107,602,707,791 people have been born on the earth. As of this writing, it is estimated that nearly seven billion people inhabit the planet. The specific estimate is 6,987,000,000. Imagine all of those books of life! As I meditated upon these things that day, I was actually stunned and laid on my bed praising the Lord and thanking Him for the privilege that He was giving me to ascend into the Father's house. I thanked the Lord, and within my heart a desire to return to the Lord's presence was birthed. I had an internal desire to thank the Lord personally. By the time I had finished reading and thinking about everything that I had experienced over the past few months, it was well into the afternoon.

It was cold and grey outside, and I decided to take another hot bath. I filled the tub again and soaked in the presence of the Lord for a long time. When I finished, I dressed and stepped into the bedroom to comb my hair. As I was looking at myself in the mirror on the door, the Lord spoke to me saying, "Kevin, come up here." For the third day in a row, I positioned myself in the little prayer closet and began to earnestly pray. This is often how I pray: I lay down and rest or luxuriate in the presence of the Lord in the same way that I do when I lay at Jesus' feet in the heavenly places. You should try it. This kind of prayer can be life-changing in ways that I do not fully understand.

## DILIGENT PRAYER

Some call this "soaking prayer," but really it is just waiting on the Lord. I purpose in my heart to still my carnal mind. I try to keep my mind and emotions from running in all directions. I found that it was helpful to pray in the Holy Spirit. Praying in the Spirit brings my mind into subjection to my spirit. It is important to be diligent in prayer. From this point, I perceive the voice of the Lord and comprehend supernatural things more easily. I prayed for a while and gave the Lord thanksgiving. I allowed my prayers to go up with praise, and I gave the Lord thanks for allowing me to visit Him in Heaven. I began to thank the Lord for allowing me to return to Him again. After a few moments, I could feel the familiar sensation of my spirit rising up.

Almost immediately I was launched heavenward, and I smiled as I understood that I was being allowed to come to Jesus in the heavens again. I knew that I was going to be with the Lord soon. I went through the same process: I landed on the stone pathway; the same two angels were there to greet me and cushion my landing. It seemed that they had been expecting me. I once again vaulted up the secret stairs to enter into the Father's house. I paid little attention to the beautiful gardens below and the crystal clear river that flowed in the distance, but I could smell the flowers and plants as I ran up the stone stairs. The angelic doorkeeper smiled at me as I breezed past him and bolted into the bathroom to be cleansed. I was given yet another new robe from the angelic attendant there. Once again I was in awe of the translucence of the material and smoothness of the robe.

I flew down the hallway of faith and ran down the circular stairway leading to the great banquet hall. Entering the great banquet hall, I looked for Jesus. He was seated at our usual table, and once again He waved at me. I threw both hands up and shouted loudly, "Praise the Lord!" My words echoed through the massive vaulted ceiling, and I saw two angels turn from their chores to smile at me. I ran to Jesus as fast as my feet could carry me.

As I entered into the presence of Jesus, I was overcome as the power and love of the Messiah and the glory of God washed over me in waves. When I reached the Lord, I fell on my face at the Lord's feet once more to worship Jesus. I luxuriated at the Lord's feet for a long time that afternoon. I just wanted to be with Him.

After some time, one of the four angels helped me stand, and I sat down in the place that had been prepared for me. Jesus and I broke bread together again, and we laughed and smiled at one another during our time in the great banquet hall. I thanked the Lord and talked to Him about many of the things that were on my heart that day. Later the Lord arose and walked purposely to the hidden door in the great banquet hall. We walked down the hallway and into the reading room preceded by the other four angelic beings that always accompanied the Lord and me. The Lord took up His usual position in His reading chair. The four angels took up their places, and the two guardian angels in the reading room greeted me with a familiar stern smile. I took a moment to scan the room again.

By the grace of God, I was able to visit this area of the Father's house on numerous occasions. Each time I entered the reading room, the Lord allowed me to learn something new and exciting about His Kingdom. So as I walked around inspecting the room more closely, I was also wondering what He would show or reveal to me this afternoon. I noticed that even though the room and its contents were obviously ancient, there was no dirt or dust. In fact, when I reflected upon this, I realized that I had not seen any dirt in any of the rooms of the great grey stone mansion that I had been visiting. This thought brought a smile to my face, and I leaned over and picked up the edge of my white robe to inspect it. It was perfectly clean. *Amazing,* I thought, *Heaven is perfectly clean!* Later I would understand that it is one of the duties of God's angelic host to keep the heavenly realms clean and perfectly maintained.

## ANOTHER VAULT ROOM

As these thoughts were percolating in my mind, the Lord called me to Himself and instructed me to follow the two guardian angels. As He was saying this, the two angels approached the Lord and acknowledged His command with a slight bow. Jesus pointed to one of the vault doors in the southeast section of the reading room. The two angels escorted me to the vault, walking at a deliberate pace. When we reached the vault door, I found it to be similar to the one that the captain guardian angel opened the day before. This vault door was the same size. It was immense and was also fashioned of what appeared to be platinum.

The captain or leader of these two strong angels stepped forward again and manipulated the various wheels and knobs that protruded from the face of the vault door. I could once again see the fire in the reading room reflecting from the highly polished metal of the door. There was the sound of clicking, and I could hear the bearings and the mechanism of the vault as they began to open under the angel's hands. I heard the same sound of a hermetic seal being broken and air rushed passed my head again. Only this time the smell of the air was more sterile in aroma. This surprised me, and as the door opened, bright light flooded into the reading room. The two guardian angels took up positions on the left and right of the open vault door to reveal an opening about fifteen feet wide and about twenty-four feet tall.

I looked at the massive door and realized that it was nearly three feet thick. I was looking at the mechanisms of the door when a voice interrupted my inspection. "You are welcome in this place." I looked up to see another pair of normal-size angels standing at the entrance to the vault door. These two angels were shorter than the other two guardian angels. These two angels had beautiful white wings and were only slightly taller than me. They were very beautiful and both had long, curly blond hair. They stepped aside in unison making a space for me to enter into the area behind the door. As I stepped through the opening, I realized that I was entering into a storage area. Immediately I knew that the room was sterile. And it had the appearance and atmosphere of a medical facility.

The two angels seemed to be very excited that I was entering the sealed room. Somehow I understood that other people had been here before me, but I also felt that it had been a while since the two angels had received a visitor. The angel who seemed to be the leader of the two spoke to me, "Please feel free to look around. This place will always be here in your times of need." This statement struck me as a little odd. I did not understand what the angel meant. Slowly I walked farther into the room. Because of the seemingly sterile environment, I was hesitant to touch anything. I thought, *I need to be careful not to contaminate these things.* When this thought came into my mind, the angel who had spoken to me said, "You need not be concerned. You are welcome here and may have whatever you wish from this place." This really surprised me and gave me pause.

I was concerned because of the items that were stored here so methodically. Before me were endless rows of neatly arranged shelves. They were perhaps fifty feet tall and each row was perhaps a hundred yards long. There were hundreds of rows of shelves. Upon each shelve was what appeared to be stainless steel containers and trays of various sizes. There were also crystal clear jars or vessels. There must have been millions upon millions of these.

## HUMAN BODY PARTS

Each stainless steel tray held human body parts. At first this caused me to be a little alarmed. But once again the angel said, "You need not be concerned. You are welcome here and may have whatever you wish from this place." When he said that for the second time, revelation began to well up from my spirit. This was the vault of spare body parts, and they would be released to people on earth who needed them. This understanding was astounding and overwhelmed my mind—I smiled broadly. At that moment the angel said, "You may have whatever you wish from this place. Please look at these and touch them if you wish. You are welcome here."

With the angel's permission, I began to look at the body parts more carefully. There were fingers, hands, thumbs, tips of fingers, arms, legs, ears, noses, and other exterior body parts in one section. In another I saw inner ears, eyeballs, veins, arteries, and nerves arranged and cataloged in a precise and very neat order. The eyeballs were stored in pairs or as individual units, each in their own crystal jar or vessel. In another section I saw skeletal parts and various bones and parts of the skeleton. In another section I saw organs. There were hearts, livers, lungs, kidneys, bladders, intestines, and so on. I remember thinking that there are a lot of people back on earth who could really use these. In another section I saw containers filled with volumes of blood and what appeared to be bone marrow. Somehow I knew that these items held the key for healing many people on earth who are battling AIDS/HIV.

When this thought came into my mind, the angel said, "Freely you have received, freely you may give" (see Matt. 10:7-8). This comment also bewildered me to a great extent, but I continued my tour of this area of the library. I took a stainless steel container down off a shelf and placed it on the table; I saw legs that appeared to belong to infants and toddlers. As I touched these items, I understood that these were body parts for children who were afflicted with paralytic diseases on earth. There were perfectly formed infant hands and feet, too. These arms, legs, fingers, toes, and lips in Heaven could be the key to their healing on earth. I picked up jars that contained eyes of various colors, and I was intrigued. I wondered who these were meant for, and I realized that there were people who needed a new eye or pair of eyes back on earth. It was a little strange to have an eyeball stare back at me from the jars. I was surprised when I noticed that the pupils of the eyes in the crystal containers seemed to dilate when I looked at them.

I held hearts that were ever so slightly beating in my hands. I looked through the vault for hours until it occurred to me that I needed to return to the Lord in the reading room. By then I had twisted and turned up and down so many rows of shelves that I could no longer see the door to the reading room. I placed a small infant heart back on the shelf in front of me, in its specified place, and looked around to my right. I wondered, *How am I going to get out of here?* At that instant, the angel tapped me on my left shoulder and said; "Follow me." I followed the angel and his associate through the maze of aisles of shelves. In a few moments, I saw the entrance and the vault door.

As I was preparing to leave, the angel waved goodbye to me and repeated, "You are always welcome here. You may have whatever you wish from this place." The angel waved and smiled graciously at me as I prepared to step back through the door. I waved back to the angel. For an instant our eyes locked, and I realized that this angel was free to deliver any of the body parts that I had seen to individuals on earth. I thought, *I hope I see these guys someday back on earth.* When this thought crossed my mind, both angels smiled broadly as if to confirm that I would be seeing them in the future.

I walked through the door and watched as the two guardian angels closed the vault door and sealed it with mechanisms that I did not comprehend. There was a "whoosh" of air, and I turned to see Jesus just as He put down a large book that He had been reading. He smiled at me and motioned me to join Him.

## RELEASING CREATIVE MIRACLES

When I reached the Lord, He was also smiling broadly. As I sat down He said, "The two angels that you saw are anointed to work with my servants upon the earth. There are many more of my angelic servants like the two you met today. From now on they will be available to assist you as you pray for My people. They can work with you to release creative miracles to those who need creative miracles in their bodies. At times they will be released to co-labor with my friends as they are anointed with the gifts of healings and miracles. Remember what you have seen and heard here today. The time is coming when My people will be released to minister in the gifts of miracles and healings in a new and greater level. My angels, like the ones you just saw, will play a role in the release of these gifts of the Holy Spirit. Prepare yourself for this, and when the time is right, I will open the door for you to tell My people to be ready for this."

The Lord and I spoke about angels and creative miracles for a bit more. After a while Jesus seemed to be satisfied that I understood Him clearly, and then the Lord stood up and we left the reading room and walked out into the gardens. As we walked, I pondered the things that I had seen and heard my heart. Later in 2002, I had an opportunity to work with healing angels like the two I met in the vault of body parts. Angels like the two in the vault help to release creative miracles, and many of these kinds of God's angels are available for anyone to work with today—that includes you.

You can co-labor with God's angels to release creative miracles. During a missions trip in 2003, the missions team and I prayed for a man named Leonard—he received a new eyeball. That well-documented creative miracle was a direct result of angelic ministry released through angelic beings like the two I met in the vault of body parts. That testimony is outlined in Chapter 12 of *Dancing with Angels 1,* Healing Angels and the Mantle for Creative Miracles. Healing angels like this have also played a role in releasing creative miracles in healing the deaf as is documented in Chapter 11, Healing Angels, in *Dancing with Angels 1.*

In the next chapter, I share several testimonies that describe other areas of Heaven including Psalm 23, the Lord's manicured gardens, and the fountain of living water.

## ENDNOTE

1. *Population Reference Bureau* article, "How Many People Have Ever Lived on Earth," 2011; http://www.prb.org/Articles/2002/HowManyPeopleHaveEverLivedonEarth.aspx; accessed March 22, 2012.

# CHAPTER 11

# EXPLORING PSALM 23
# THE RIVER OF REVELATION

*Written in February 2002*

Tonight, just a few minutes ago, the Lord spoke to me. It is not unusual for Jesus to speak to me like this. Sometimes I am allowed to enter into the realms of Heaven. The Lord sometimes invites me into His very presence. Many times I have dined with Jesus in the great banquet hall. Sometimes Jesus invites me to explore the different rooms and places in His Father's great mansion (see John 14:2). The Lord has also been allowing me to explore the vast areas and lands that are surrounding the beautiful stone mansion and its manicured gardens.

There are hundreds of thousands of square miles in this beautiful heavenly land around the glorious home that Jesus is allowing me to tour. One of my most favorite places to go is the beautiful green meadows by the still, crystal clear waters. One of my favorite things to do in that place is to simply lie at the feet of Jesus. We usually do this after dinner in the great banquet hall. I ask Jesus to allow me to sit with Him by the still waters and listen to His sayings, or just luxuriate in His glory. We then leave the banquet hall and walk down a great winding, grey stone walkway that leads to the gardens and fountains of life therein. We are always accompanied by four friendly angels who serve the Lord and see to our needs by ministering to us in various ways.

I often ask the Lord to go to the still waters by the crystal river of God. There the angels will have prepared a place for us. There is a beautiful blanket or ornate quilts waiting for us, spread out on the soft, green grass. I recline at the feet of Jesus on one and bask in the heavenly sunshine. The Lord speaks to me, and I listen quietly to His sayings. In this place I am totally content, just being in the presence of Jesus.

## THE RIVER OF LIFE

The still waters are the waters of life. These are the waters of Psalm 23, and they flow crystal clear and silently through the heart of this heavenly place. They flow forth from the throne of God and of the Lamb who is found in the crystal cathedral in Heaven (see Rev. 22:1). They are the waters of the river in the Garden of Eden. They are the healing waters of Ezekiel 47. They are the healing waters of Psalm 23. They are the healing waters of Revelation 22. They are the waters of Psalm 46. They are the waters of Numbers 20:11. This beautiful, crystal clear water meanders by the fruitful meadows in this place, Psalm 23. The Lord has allowed me to freely dive into the crystal clear depths of the river of life.

This river of life is clear and warm. Beside the banks of this river grow beautiful trees of all kinds, and they continually bear fruit. These trees are always in full bloom, and they also have ripe fruit at all times. The trees provide for the needs of the people in this wonderful place. These perfect trees are beautiful beyond compare, and they forever release a wonderful heavenly aroma. The sensation when smelling their fragrance is like smelling a fresh-baked, hot apple pie coming right out of the oven. My mouth begins to water and my spirit begins to soar when I behold the beauty and fragrance of these trees. There are thousands upon thousands of trees like this that line the river of life in this heavenly place (see Rev. 22:2).

In the river of life have I made many discoveries. There I have found treasures. Jesus has allowed me to keep many of these heavenly things. Once, Jesus Himself swam with me in the still waters of the river of life. On the dive, I showed the Lord a sunken treasure chest that I had discovered on a previous expedition. The treasure chest lies in about seventy feet of water near a bend in the river of life, and is full of treasures. It has thousands of precious gemstones and other articles hidden in the chest.

When Jesus free-dived with me, He chose a very large and multi-faceted diamond for me from the depths of the sunken chest. It was a brilliant crystal clear gem. When we inspected the diamond in the radiant sunshine of the Psalm 23 meadow, a cascade of colors radiated from this perfectly cut heavenly gem. When Jesus rotated the gem in His hand, it sent out an array of luminous colors throughout the area, and revelation flowed into my spirit instantaneously. At other times I have taken jewels from the hidden trove, but none have been as magnificent as the one that Jesus gave to me. Once I found a small diamond and another time I found a very small but brilliant red ruby.

When I show these heavenly gemstones to Jesus, He always gives me some new revelation. On another occasion when I was diving with Jesus in the river of life, He directed me to a small pouch. I somehow knew that the pouch was a very ancient coin purse. It is about the size of my hand and is closed by a leather band. The Lord uses these things to reveal to me some of the hidden treasures of Heaven and His Kingdom (see Prov. 25:2). When the Lord gave me the coin purse, Jesus and I ascended through the crystal clear waters about seventy feet to the surface of the waters of life. When we arrived at the shore, the four angels were waiting for us with us two immaculate white towels and the angels helped us dry ourselves. Then we returned to our beautiful quilts and sat in the warming sunshine.

I have seen these angels many times before. These are the same four angels that were with Jesus when He called me to come to Him in Heaven the first time. I know them. They are gentle and meek and walk in humility much like Christ. The first one that I was introduced to has beautiful blond, shoulder length hair. This angel has bright, piercing blue eyes. Jesus has allowed me to work with this angel before in order to see my prayers answered. That is an amazing feeling when Jesus allows you to loose an angel and then you see the results of the answered prayers bringing needed things, or healing, or revelation and such!

## DIAMONDS AND WEAPONS

Later, Jesus took the purse from me and showed me the "combination" needed to open it. He handed it to me smiling and with a great deal of satisfaction. It seemed that the Lord was very happy to be giving these heavenly treasures away. When I looked inside the pouch I discovered that it contained twelve perfect diamonds. They were identical in shape, clarity, and cut. The diamonds were perfect and spotless. Somehow I knew that they represented Christ's spotless bride. The diamonds were about the size of a man's thumb, and would be extremely valuable on earth. Priceless!

I have found other treasures in the river of life. These include a beautiful two-edged sword. This sword fit my hand as if it had been tailor-made for my grip. The sword of the Lord is of the finest workmanship and fashioned of the finest gold. The blade has fine, inlaid work and is obviously of heavenly manufacture. It is light as a feather and as sharp as a laser. The Lord has instructed me to use this weapon of warfare in the prayer ministry and in intercession on occasion. The Holy Spirit will often lead me to unsheathe the sword to cut off hindrances from those whom I have prayed for. I have used the sword to surgically remove generational curses, and associated demonic spirits. The sword of the Lord is especially effective when it is used in this manner. Spirits of infirmity, the spirit of death, and suicide are loosed as the sword cuts and frees. At other times it is used to dismember demonic beings, breaking their assignments, and freeing people in various ministry settings and places on earth.

On another occasion, I found a beautiful, small, golden dagger. It had a large, round ruby encased in the end of its handle. This is a spiritual weapon of warfare, and I know that it has been hidden for many centuries. The Lord will give His people many of these kinds of powerful weapons in the coming season (see 2 Cor. 10:4).

On the day that Jesus gave me the twelve perfect diamonds, He started to show me things in His Kingdom. I stayed at the feet of Jesus for a long time that afternoon by the still waters of Psalm 23. We allowed the gentle breeze to dry our hair and the white robes we were wearing. The Lord was glad that I was near Him and allowed me to lie at His feet for a long time. I soaked in the presence of Jesus, adoring the Lamb of God. I could smell the wonderful heavenly fragrance of the Lord. The fragrance of His presence smells like a mixture of frankincense and roses. I could also smell the fragrance of the flora and fauna that grows in abundance beside the river of life. Heaven.

In this lovely region of Psalm 23, there is a profusion of flowers. There are so many different flowers that I cannot begin to name them all. Somehow I know that there are varieties of flowers in this heavenly place that do not grow on earth. But there are also some of the most beautiful roses and majestic sunflowers that I have ever seen. I have also knelt on my hands and knees gazing at the most spectacular purple lilies of the field in the meadows of Psalm 23. The aroma that these ethereal flowering plants produce is truly mesmerizing and actually intoxicating.

I have observed that as the Lord Jesus walks past these flowers that they actually turn toward the Son of God, just as flowers on earth turn to face the sun in the heavens too. The flowers worship the Christ as He passes by. Even the grass seems to worship the Savior. Occasionally a gently breeze or zephyrs flow through Psalm 23; and when this happens, it seems that even the trees worship Jesus as they appear to clap their leaves together. Even the stones cry out in this incredible place (see Luke 19:40).

## ENJOYING THE CHILDREN

This day there was a large group of small children that came to play beside the Lord and me as I basked in the presence of the Son. The Lord rose and began to dance, sing, and play with the children. I stayed on the blanket and observed them for some time. Jesus loves the little children, and He was so happy to be in their presence. They smiled and laughed as they played ring around the rosy. After a time I joined them, and we all danced by the river of life as we were dancing with Jesus. Even the angels joined in our circle and danced with us singing and praising God! While we danced and laughed, the bright green clover tickled between my toes as we played in our bare feet. What a happy and joyful time that was.

These precious children had no cares and were content and full of life and the love of God. Somehow I was aware that many of these children had come to Heaven as fetuses who had been aborted before they could live their God-ordained lives. Others were precious children who had been lost by grieving parents. After a while, these children of the Most High moved on through the meadow chasing a colorful swarm of butterflies (see Ps. 82:6). The butterflies they were chasing were mind-blowing in their colors. They actually radiated hues I have never witnessed on earth. They floated freely by on the gentle breezes in the meadow of Psalm 23, and the children enjoy an eternal game of chase with these ethereal creatures.

The Lord and I lay back down and rested on the blankets, and He was smiling at me graciously. As mentioned previously, the blankets, or quilts, were incredible—intricately sewn and made of the finest fabrics. They are brightly colored and made of a patchwork of silks and other fine materials. The four friendly angels always prepare a place for us in the Psalm 23 meadow, and they always unroll these incredibly beautiful blankets for the Lord and me to rest upon. Not only are the blankets that we use for our picnics soft, but they smell like frankincense, too. It is a joy when they touch my skin and when their fragrance reaches my nose! I love to lie at the feet of Jesus on those heavenly blankets.

## WALKING WITH JESUS

Sometimes the Lord invites me to go for long walks with Him. I love to walk with Jesus. I know that He will show me some new places and give me more revelation of the places around the Father's mansion. This day, Jesus smiled at me and took my left hand in His as He began to lead me. This was the first time that I had looked closely and studied the scars of His hands. Jesus allowed me to place my index finger into the indention where the nail pierced His palm. He was very patient with me. Somehow I knew that many had done the same thing. I took the forefinger of my right hand and traced the outline of the wound. When I did this, the reality of His sacrifice for me brought tears to my eyes. Jesus reached out with His right hand and gently wiped away my tears. This brought a smile to my face again.

Then the Lord led me back to the bank of the river of life that meanders through the grassy meadow of Psalm 23. I thought that Jesus may have wished to dive back into the depths of the water again. He did not. He said, "Come with me." *It is a good idea to follow Jesus.* When we reached the edge of the water, Jesus simply stepped out onto the water and began to walk on the river. This was not a surprise to me because I have witnessed the Lord walk across the still waters here many times before. What surprised me was I was also walking on the waters with Him. Jesus held my left hand gently in His nail-scarred right hand and gently led me out onto the crystal clear waters of the river of life. I could feel the cool water on the soles of my bare feet. I looked up at Jesus in surprise to see a beaming smile crease His face reassuring me.

As we walked across the river of life, I noticed that our four angelic friends were waving at us from the arched wooden bridge that spans the river in this section of the Psalm 23 meadow. They waved and smiled, and I smiled back; somehow I knew that they would be meeting the Lord and me in a little while. The bridge is beautiful yet simple. I know that it is thousands of years old, yet it is in immaculate condition. Colorful flowers meet its base on each end and there is a stone walkway that leads to and from it in this place. That walkway eventually leads up to the Father's mansion and also through the Lord's gardens. The pathway also passes by the waters in the garden. Sometimes I stop there and an angel will give me a clean crystal goblet to drink from. The water at the waters is always fresh, clear, and refreshing.

The Lord told me that He wanted to show me something. When we reached the other side of the river of life, He took me up to a very high mountain. When we reached the top, we sat together on a large stone bench. It was about twenty-four inches high and about eighteen inches wide. The view from there was breathtaking. We could see for hundreds of miles in every direction. This is Heaven—it is beautiful beyond words. I was in awe. I sat with Jesus in silence for a long while just taking in as much of the view as I could. I was mesmerized by the beauty of this place. The mountains here were truly colossal; I doubt there are any mountains this immense upon the earth. I soaked in the love and majesty of the Lord as I gazed upon the incredible view before us. I knew that this was a very special place. It is a secret place. It is the secret place of the Most High. I took the time to examine the vista in all 360 degrees around us. Off to the south in the great distance I could make out a massive and well-manicured vineyard. I had a knowing that it was also a very special place.

I had a revelation that I would return to be with Jesus in this place in the future. But I put that out of my thoughts as it seemed that the Lord wanted me to look at the vineyard. It was the reason for our hike to the summit of the mountain. Jesus asked me, "Would you like to see My Father's vineyard?" I immediately agreed, "Yes, Lord." and asked the Lord to take me there.

What you are about to read now took place over the course of several days and several visits to the Lord in the heavenly places. It never occurred to me to write these experiences down, nor did I ever have any intention to do so. I had purposed to keep them treasured within my heart. I would not have written any of this had it not been for the Lord bidding me to do so. Let me share with you the things that Jesus showed me in the manicured gardens, and in the Father's vineyard during that season.

# CHAPTER 12

# THE LORD'S
# MANICURED GARDENS

I entered my little prayer room in desperation. Recently, I had done this many times as the cares of this world had weighed heavily upon me. The frustrations of a busy work day clung to me like a spider's web, and I longed to be in the presence of the Lord. Even though I was still hot and sweaty, I knelt down and began to pray. It was just past 3 o'clock on a sunny, hot afternoon. This seemed like just another time of seeking God's face. However, as I called on the name of the Lord, His presence began to envelop me, washing away the cares of my day—and something very special began to unfold.

As the anointing of the Holy Spirit and the love of God met me in my little prayer closet, I began to weep as something precious bubbled up from some deep and forgotten place within me. The presence of the Lord began to refresh me again. I fell prostrate on the old shag carpet. The glory of God began to wash over me in waves. Unexpectedly, I found myself under a heavy weighty blanket of glory, and it felt as if warm sand had glued me to the prayer room floor. I was no longer able to move my body as the tangible presence of the Lord seemed to bond me to the carpet.

I simply luxuriated in His presence and tears flowed freely from my eyes. What a precious thing it was to feel the love of Jesus wash over me this way. I laid there in His presence for the longest time. It may have been hours, I really don't know. I was lost in God's presence when suddenly a familiar sensation began to spring up from within my body. Once again I could feel my spirit as it seemed to launch up through the ceiling of my little prayer room.

When I opened my eyes, I could see the little house at 121 Beech Street as it grew smaller below me. In the twilight I could see the lights of the city twinkling and growing more distant beneath me. It seemed as if my spirit was being hurled through the atmosphere, and I passed supernaturally higher and higher until I could see the planet Earth far below. In an instant I was shooting between the planets, through the stars—and finally I entered the tunnel light. It seemed as if I was traveling at the speed of light.

As I accelerated through the tunnel, brilliant phosphorescent colors blurred past me at incredible speeds. I looked to my left to see an angel smile at me. This angelic escort was holding my left hand and he was helping orchestrate this trip into the heavenly places. However, I was not the least bit frightened because I had been in this place before. I had seen this angel before, and I knew where he was leading me. In fact, I relaxed and enjoyed the sensation as my spirit was launched through the supernatural tunnel of mesmerizing lights. The feeling was wonderful, and the abiding presence and love of Christ continued to wrap me in a warm blanket of His love.

My spirit continued to accelerate supernaturally through this tunnel of light and the experience lasted for quite a while. I twisted, turned, and traveled through time and space as my spirit was being sucked through the supernatural tunnel. After a time, the tunnel curved and I could see a familiar place in the distance. As I flew out from the end of the tunnel, much like water pouring out from a faucet, I landed on my hands and knees.

Immediately, four angels gathered around me to help me stand upright. They were all taller than me and radiated the love of God. They smiled at me gently as they helped me to my feet. I was a little wobbly. I looked into each angel's beautiful eyes. What lovely and caring eyes these angels have. I looked at each one in turn and each one smiled at me greeting me and making me feel totally secure, safe, and welcome in this place. I had been to this place before.

My angelic friends were all dressed in immaculate white garments. After I looked into their eyes, I looked down at my feet and noticed that I was robed in a white garment, too. My feet were bare and I stood on the beautiful stone pathway. I had seen this pathway before and I knew that it leads up to the Father's house and to the place I call the great banquet hall.

The amazing thing about these stone walkways in this place is that each stone fits perfectly into the next and there is no mortar in the seams. In the past, I've actually gotten down on my hands and knees to examine these pathways carefully. I could not find any chisel or tool marks, and the stones were perfectly smooth. Each stone is perfectly and precisely joined to the next in a way that is not humanly possible. They are made of a beautiful light-colored stone and were cool under the soles of my bare feet. These pathways are amazing works of art.

On either side of the stone pathways are the Lord's manicured gardens. The grass is meticulously trimmed; in fact, it appeared to me that the grass was living as I had walked on these pathways in the past with the Lord. It seemed as if the grass and the tiny flowers therein would turn and follow the Son of God as He passed by. They were attracted to Jesus. I found this quite amazing and went to great pains to observe how the grass and flowers turned toward Jesus as He walked by. I had invested hours in the past just examining the magnificent tiny flowers in the grasses in these heavenly gardens. Even the tiniest flowers have a wonderful aroma.

As I took my eyes from my feet and looked into the faces of the four angels around me, they smiled once more and waved goodbye. And I found myself alone on the pathway of God. Off to my left I saw the stone stairway that leads up to the mansion. I often ascend that stairway to be with the Lord Jesus and dine with Him in the great banquet hall. The stones of that stairway are also perfect and many beautiful flowers and vines grow near that walkway. Ahead of me and in the distance I could see the glory of God as it hovered around the mountains there. These magnificent mountain ranges are hundreds of miles away, but the air is so crystal clear here and these heavenly mountains are very easy to see even at this distance. They radiated a majestic, royal purple hue in the heavenly light.

## HIS ROSE GARDEN

Farther down to my right I saw the gardens. The Lord Jesus had taken me into those gardens before and had shown me an area where He has thousands of manicured rose bushes. That time, Jesus and I invested a whole day just looking at all the different colored roses. We smelled them and then the Lord smiled at me with great delight when He would find one that was especially pleasing to Him. During the tour of the rose garden, I was surprised at how tenderly and intimately Christ knew each plant. In fact, God loves every plant and longs for each one to bear beautiful flowers (see John 15:5,8).

The Lord's rose garden is carefully tended and manicured by angelic beings. These angels are gardeners and they are assigned to keep God's gardens manicured and in perfect shape. The angels work in the Lord's rose gardens year round because the grounds are so massive. I found it amazing that the angels were not in the least bit dirty and their robes were always perfectly white and clean. Obviously these angelic gardeners are very good at what they do. I believe that at times God sends angels like this to earth to help people with their crops. Perhaps that is what happened in situations like the one portrayed in the movie *Faith Like Potatoes?*

As Jesus and I were leaving the rose garden that day, I passed near one of these gardening angels. At that instant it occurred to me that I was seeing a member of the great cloud of witnesses (see Heb. 12:1). This angel smiled at me and there was tenderness and a love that exuded from its presence. I had an understanding that this angel or this member of the great cloud of witnesses had once been a gardener on earth. In fact, gardening was its passion in life and the work it is doing in the Lord's garden was the fulfillment of the desires of his heart (see Ps. 37:4). The angel smiled at me a second time and nodded as if to confirm what I was feeling.

As I passed by, the thought occurred to me that when I'm absent from my body (die), the Lord will allow me to pursue a passion that I loved while on the earth (see 2 Cor. 5:8). At that moment gentle breeze blew my robe and ruffled my hair, and I could smell the river that runs through the garden. As my attention was drawn to that beautiful crystal clear river, another thought came into my mind. *Perhaps I could be like this gardener, but instead of caring for the Lord's rose gardens I should oversee the river of life and invest my days fishing there in Heaven.* A big smile grew across my face with this thought and I turned to see Jesus smiling at me in agreement. These memories of my past visits to the gardens of the Lord began to fade, and I found myself alone on the path to the garden. I continued to walk and enjoy the sights, sounds, and smells of Heaven along the way.

I found myself looking down across the gardens as the four angels were going their own separate ways. They had come to help me, to greet me, and to welcome me again. I took a deep breath and inhaled perfectly pure air into my lungs. I could smell the wonderful fragrances of the flowers that grew in abundance in that special place. I stood there for moment taking it all in. Every single one of my five senses was on overload! It was such a pleasure to be back in the Lord's gardens, and I noticed for the first time the sound of ethereal angelic worship was lingering in the air around me. The air was alive in this special place; it was endued with the power and the presence of the Lord Jesus. Even the sky radiated the presence and love of God in Heaven.

## THE LION OF JUDAH

I smiled and began to walk along the perfectly manicured path. I had walked about one hundred yards on the path of God just examining my surroundings when I saw some movement to my left. I stopped to see what it was. For a moment my heart leapt into my throat as I saw a large male lion rise up and stretch. As this massive lion yawned, I could see its fangs; however, I did not feel threatened by this beast. Nevertheless, I was very surprised to see a lion on the loose in this place.

He was absolutely beautiful as he stretched out on his front paws and arched his back up into the evening sunshine. The heavenly light glistened off of the lion's golden mane and for a moment it seemed to actually glow! He yawned broadly again and began to leisurely walk toward me slowly wagging his tail. I stood frozen on the stone pathway with my heart beating within my chest. I was aware of the coolness of the stones against my bare feet. The lion continued to walk toward me looking at me face to face. His beautiful mane was ruffled by a gentle breeze as he stared into my eyes for a fleeting second. This celestial lion had beautiful yellow eyes that radiated the love of God. For a moment the thought entered my mind that I should run, but I knew I was safe so I continued to watch this magnificent creature as he deliberately covered the last few feet between us.

The lion walked right up to me; his head was level with my shoulders, and he looked up at me slightly—then he licked me! He licked my face with his oversized and very wet, textured tongue. Then the lion began to lick my left hand and my left arm. I reached out with my right hand and patted him on top of his massive head. He licked me a few more times. The lion was purring as he shot me a parting glance and walked away. I could have sworn that the lion smiled at me as he walked on by and settled down nearby in the shade under what looked to be a flowering magnolia tree. I took a deep breath and laughed.

As I walked down the path, I glanced over my shoulder to see my new friend lay down for another nap. I continued down the path pondering being licked by a lion and what that might mean. As I walked along, I looked at the grass and the tiny flowers that were in it. The flowers and the grass seemed to be alive; in fact, they seemed to be looking at me. So I actually got down on my hands and knees and examined them for a few minutes. I could have sworn that there were tiny voices within the grasses praising God.

After a while, I continued to amble on the pathway of the Lord and enjoy the atmosphere of Heaven. I was lost in my thoughts as I luxuriated in the majesty of this astonishing place. In my heart a desire began to spring up. The thought of walking into the gardens instead of going up into the house today came into my mind. So at the place where the path diverged, I veered to the right and started to walk down to the gardens. It was wonderful to be in this place again.

The gentle breezes carried the aromas of heaven, and angelic worship rode on the winds of paradise, too. At that moment I heard the roar of a lion behind me. When I turned to look, I saw Jesus waving at me! That really surprised me. The Lord turned away and walked up the hill. So I continued down the pathway farther into the manicured gardens. There had been a desire within my heart to explore this area of Heaven for a long time. From time to time I would stop to smell a flower or to look at some unusual plant or feature of the gardens. There are amazing assortments of exotic plants that grow in abundance along the pathways of God in the rose gardens. I was really enjoying this afternoon in Heaven and by now all the cares of my earthly day simply vanished.

## THE MAZE

As I strolled along, I came to the top of a knoll and below me I could see an extensive maze in the garden of the Lord. I had been to this place before with Jesus but now I was alone. Yet within me there was desire to go down to one of the fountains of life that is there in the center of the maze. As I entered the maze, I was once again astonished at how beautiful and how immaculately maintained the maze plants are.

The maze consists of bushes that are perfectly healthy and are covered in beautiful flowers. Each section of the maze has different colored flowers and the colors seem to blend perfectly and seamlessly together from section to section. In fact, the way the colors blend together is quite striking to behold. The colors blend together in the same way that the colors of the rainbow mesh flawlessly into one another.

The flowers gave off wonderful heavenly aromas as I walked from section to section. My sense of smell was treated to many different fragrances as I passed between them just as my eyes were tickled by the multitude of various colors. As I walked through the rows of the maze, the peace and presence of Jesus was with me, and the cares of the world were totally forgotten and left behind. I was lost in paradise.

## HEAVENLY VIPs

From time to time I would see other people walking in the maze. At one point I passed a very elderly man and woman who were strolling through the garden hand in hand. It was apparent to me that they were in love. To be as old as they seemed to be they also appeared to be in remarkably good health. They talked to one another and laughed as they strolled along. As I passed by them they looked at me and greeted me with a smile. Their beautiful blue eyes twinkled in the brilliant evening sunshine.

I realized that these two people have been in God's garden for an eternity. In my heart I desired to stop them and engage them in conversation. I was very curious and would have loved to ask them a whole bunch of questions. I was certain that they knew a lot about the Lord's garden. I wanted to find out who they were. I sensed that they were quite important, heavenly VIPs. Somehow I also knew I would be interrupting their special time together. So I simply smiled back at them and passed on by quietly. That seemed like the right thing to do.

I stopped after I had walked several yards and glanced back over my shoulder. I was drawn to them for some unknown reason, perhaps it was the anointing of the Holy Spirit that seemed to emanate from them? They continued to walk and talk in the garden. For a moment they also stopped and turned to look back at me. For a fleeting second I thought about running back to speak to them. They waved at me and smiled, then turning they continued on their way. Somehow I understood that this couple was very special God. So I chose to honor and respect their privacy and continued on my way, too.

I understood that they had been in the Lord's garden for a very long time. Perhaps, longer than anyone else save for the Trinity. I was certain of the fact that these two had a lot of revelation about this place. I wanted to talk to them about some of the hidden mysteries I had seen here in the heavenly realms. For instance, did the grass and tiny flowers in this place really worship God with their voices? The elderly couple, the heavenly VIPs, carried themselves with a sense of nobility, yet they also seemed very humble and meek. These two were truly friends of God. Somehow I had the revelation that the Lord had often walked with them in the garden in the cool of the day.

I began to wonder what things they had talked about with God. It would have been quite interesting to know, but somehow I also understood that the timing for this was not quite right. I also had a knowing that I would have an opportunity to speak to this amazing couple at my leisure in the future. After I waved to them, I dropped my right hand back down to my side. As I did, it brushed against the material of my white robe and it seemed smoother than silk. I wondered just exactly what kind of material it was. I had so many questions about this place. I suppose that it would take an eternity to have them all answered. I continued walking through the maze of the Lord's garden lost in my thoughts and meandering on the pathways of God. I began to grow thirsty, so I headed toward the fountains of life for a drink of living water.

CHAPTER 13

# THE FOUNTAIN OF
# THE WATER OF LIFE

I walked through the garden for what seemed like hours. The same presence and the same glory and love of God that had rested upon me in my prayer room was still upon me now as I walked in the garden in the cool of the day. As I made my way through the maze, I knew my destination was the fountain of living water. I had been to that special place before. In fact, Jesus had taken me to this particular fountain one of the first times I had come to be with Him in these heavenly places during this special season (see Eph. 3:10). There are many fountains like this one in the realms of Heaven.

On that day, the Messiah and I had left the great banquet hall and we had walked down the stone stairway from the back of the great banquet hall together. That winding stone stairway leads down to the stone pathways on which I was walking now. Those pathways meander freely throughout the Lord's gardens, and eventually they lead to the fountain of living water. It is a very nice walk, quite refreshing; I hope you will enjoy it sometime, too. When the Lord and I had come to the waters that day, there were many people fellowshipping around the fountain. And they all seemed very glad that Jesus had come to be with them.

The Lord and I walked over and sat on the edge of the fountain because it makes a good bench. In fact, I think that it was designed that way, as a place for folks to rest and refresh themselves. The fountain is amazing. The fountain of living water is about sixty feet or more in diameter and the top of the fountain is about forty-five feet high. It is quite large. This one is set in the center of the gardens and is a real focal point of this region of the heavenly realms. I guess that is why it is positioned in the center of the Lord's manicured gardens.

Many people come to drink of the crystal clear waters that flow from the top of the fountain. The Lord showed me that the waters come from the river of God. I understand that the river of God is the same river that flows from the very throne room of the Father. This is described very well in Revelation chapter 22. I believe the first two verses of that chapter are all about the river of God I had seen, swam in, and tasted:

> *And he showed me a pure river of water of life, clear as crystal, proceeding from the throne of God and of the Lamb. In the middle of its street, and on either side of the river, was the tree of life, which bore twelve fruits, each tree yielding its fruit every month. The leaves of the tree were for the healing of the nations* (Revelation 22:1-2).

In fact, the river of God is also the same river that flows through the meadow of Psalm 23. That is the place where those healing trees are flourishing and always in bloom. These healing trees remind me of the majestic magnolia trees on earth, but the flowers of the heavenly trees have much larger blooms and flowers. Those blooms permeate the air in the meadow of Psalm 23 with an exquisite aroma that is quite delicious; in fact, you can actually taste the fragrance! I will describe that in more detail later, but the fountain of life is just exquisite!

The fountains are made of beautiful white stones and just like the pathways in the garden there seems to be no mortar or tool marks from the fountain's construction. The white stones are immaculate and the water within the fountain is crystal clear. In fact, it seems to be alive.

In the center of the fountain of living water is a tower, and from the top of that place the crystal clear water bubbles out. It bubbles out like an artesian well, but I am sure that its source is the river of God. The holy water flows majestically down from intricately carved basins to the next intricately carved basins below. It flows down from the top from intricately carved basins to the larger pool where Jesus and I were seated on the wide ledge.

This ledge is the perfect size to sit on and relax and be refreshed by the living water. It is about twenty-four inches wide and is also made of the same immaculate white stone. As the water tumbles down, it makes delightful sounds that mingle with the ethereal sounds of harps, flutes, and various other stringed instruments. The sound at the fountain of living water is extremely peaceful as angelic singing and worship mingle with the sounds of the falling waters of life. Here even the fountain of living water worships the Messiah.

On this particular day, I was sitting beside the fountain of living water with Jesus. The Lord made a motion with His right hand signaling an angel who was nearby to come over to us. The angel carried a serving tray made of the finest materials and he handed to the Lord a beautiful crystal clear goblet. Jesus took the goblet and with His left hand He held it out so that the living water from the fountain of life trickled into it from one of the intricately carved lower basins, filling the crystal clear goblet with the crystal clear water of life. When it was full, Jesus extended the goblet to me. The water is perfectly pure and holy.

With His left hand, the Lord handed me the goblet with the crystal clear, pure water. As Jesus stretched forth His hand, I could see the place where the nails had pierced His body and for a moment tears filled my eyes and a deep sense of sadness welled up from within my spirit again. At that instant it became silent near the fountain of living water and I was aware of the fact that the people and angels nearby were looking at us. More precisely they were looking at me with great sympathy.

Sadness is not very common in Heaven. I reached out with my right hand and took the crystal goblet from the Messiah in this silence. When

I did, my fingertips touched His hand and the sadness that I had felt instantly disappeared. With my left hand, I quickly wiped away a tear that had escaped from my left eye. As I looked up, I saw the Messiah smiling lovingly at me. His beautiful eyes contained the unfathomable love that God for has for you and me.

When I took the goblet into my hands, I saw that very ornate designs had been carefully etched into the crystal. I studied the intricacy of the fine design in amazement for a moment. Its detail was bewildering to me as I had never seen such craftsmanship. When I glanced up, I saw the angel hand the Lord Jesus Christ a second goblet, and once again Jesus filled the glass with living water from the fountain. Once again waves of God's love washed over me. As I sat on the edge of the fountain in the presence of Jesus, I was aware of the enormity of the great sacrifice that He had made for me and for all humankind.

## DRINKING THE WATER OF LIFE

The love of God that the Messiah has for every tongue, every tribe, and every nation is impossible for us to understand with our carnal minds and human intellect. At that moment, Jesus raised His glass indicating that we should drink. As I raised the crystal goblet to my lips and began to drink the water of life, it felt as if a supernatural cleansing was taking place within my soul. As the water passed over my lips and down my esophagus and into my stomach, the power of God washed over me. I looked up to see the Messiah drinking the crystal clear water from the fountain of life, too. When He finished, the Lord handed His crystal goblet to the angel standing nearby and smiled at me.

I was aware of the fact that I could also hand my glass to the angel, but instead I had an overwhelming desire to drink deeply from the water of life. So I held the crystal goblet at the same place Jesus had, where the living water was flowing freely from the fountain of life. I filled my goblet and once again I drank freely from the living water. I did this several times, and as the Lord watched me drinking heartily, He smiled at me like a proud papa on his child's birthday.

Jesus' smile indicated that He was overjoyed that I was drinking more from the fountain of life! However, He surprised me when He began laughing heartily. And at that moment I realized that I could have as much of this precious water as I desired, at any time I was thirsty. I began to laugh too, and we sat together on the side of the fountain of life laughing heartily for a long time. Soon everyone in the area was laughing cheerfully, and the love of God enveloped me in a fresh way as I saw how the Lord was laughing and enjoying Himself by the fountain of living water.

After a few minutes, the Lord looked lovingly and intently into my eyes. The Lord held out a new crystal clear goblet that was filled with the water of life. The Messiah held it in His mighty right hand. For a moment there was a great silence, and then Jesus spoke emphatically to me. But I understood that what He was saying was for anyone who was thirsty for more of God.

The Messiah said:

*If anyone thirsts, let him come to Me and drink. Let them come to Me all you who are thirsty. I will pour water on him who is thirsty. Let everyone who is thirsty know, come to the waters; and you who have no money, come, buy, and eat. Yes, come, buy wine and milk without money and without price. For there is a fountain and whoever drinks of the water that I shall give him will never thirst. But the water that I shall give him will become in him a fountain of water springing up into everlasting life. He who believes in Me, as the Scripture has said, out of his heart will flow rivers of living water. If anyone thirsts, let him come to Me and drink. It is done! I am the Alpha and the Omega, the Beginning and the End. I will give of the fountain of the water of life freely to him who thirsts. He who overcomes shall inherit all things, and I will be his God and he shall be My son. Come! And let him who hears say, "Come!" And let him who thirsts come. Whoever desires let him take the water of life freely. He who drinks this water, out of his heart will flow rivers of living water* (see John 7:37-38).

When Jesus finished speaking, a crescendo of angelic worship instantaneously exploded in the air surrounding the Messiah, and the glory of God multiplied around us again. Jesus continued to smile lovingly at me and gazed intently into my eyes for several precious moments. We continued to sit at the fountain for a while, and I drank even more of the living water. Then we arose and walked down into the meadow of Psalm 23. Several angels accompanied us on that day, and I remember the wonderful time that we had as we broke bread together on a blanket there by the river of God.

## THIS DAY

As I was walking down the pathway this day remembering that encounter at the fountain of living water, a smile spread across my face. I recalled that experience with fondness and assurance, and I was glad that I was walking on the path of God to return to the fountain of life. Within my spirit, a desire grew within me to sit on the ledge of the fountain of life and to drink from a new crystal goblet from the water of life. After all, they flow freely from the very throne of the Father and of the Lamb, and I could have as much as I liked. And this day I was very hot and very thirsty.

A little while later I came to the spot where Jesus and I had drank freely from the fountain of life. There were several people and angels milling around in the area adjacent to the fountain of life. I sat down by myself in the exact spot where Jesus had spoken to me by the fountain of life. I closed my eyes for a few minutes and pondered these things in my heart. I realized that I had been walking for quite a while, and I had covered a long distance on this visit. It occurred to me that I was very thirsty; and as this thought passed through my mind, someone tapped me lightly on my left shoulder breaking my concentration.

I turned, and looking to my left I saw the same angel that had served Jesus and me. The angel that served us was standing beside me with a big, bright smile on his face. In his hands was the same serving tray and upon it were two crystal goblets. Suddenly the winds began to swirl around us ever so gently and I felt the presence of the Lord increase. I saw the angelic being look behind me with his piercing blue eyes. As I turned to see what he was looking at, I saw the Lord walking up to the fountain of life. I fell down on my knees and grasped His feet. I saw the nail scars.

Once again I began to weep. The Lord placed His right hand upon my head and I stood to my feet. Jesus motioned me to sit down beside Him on the ledge of the fountain of life. Once again a tear began to roll slowly down my left cheek. The Lord sat down beside me. Smiling at me, He noticed my tears and reached out with His right hand and wiped away my tears (see Isa. 25:8). When the Messiah did that, I smiled too. At that moment, the angel handed Jesus a crystal clear goblet and the Lord reached out with His left hand and filled it with the living water from the fountain of life. Then He handed it to me.

Waves of glory and love washed over me and the peace of God that passes our ability to comprehend filled my entire being. The angel offered a second crystal clear goblet to the Lord, and He also filled that one. I could feel the intricate designs that were etched into the fine crystal under my fingertips. The Lord raised His glass and we drank freely of the living water together once again. The power of God coursed through my being, and I felt the healing power of the Lord refreshing me. My ability to taste, touch, hear, smell, and feel were suddenly supernaturally multiplied. And the love of God began to well up from within my heart.

I tarried with Christ for a long time at the fountain of living water. He spoke many things into my heart that day. After a while, I knew that it was time for me to return home. I stood up beside Jesus and He looked deeply and lovingly into my eyes. He said, "You are always welcome here." Looking deeply into my eyes, the Lord told me to go now and write down all of the things that I had both seen and heard when I returned to my little house at 121 Beech Street (see Acts 4:20).

With that the Lord said goodbye, turned, and walked away down one of the paths that leads through His gardens. I sat back down on the ledge of the fountain of living water and watched the Lord as He retreated into the garden. I saw a small child run to Jesus and the Lord swept him up in His arms. They laughed and played for several minutes until the boy ran back to join the other children who were playing a game in the gardens nearby. Angels were watching over the children and attending to their every need as they laughed and played innocently in this delightful and supernatural Paradise.

I stayed upon the ledge of the fountain of living water for a long time pondering these things in my heart. *Who was that elderly couple? Who did all of those children belong to, and why were they here? Why don't more of God's people come and drink freely from the fountain of living water?* I turned to splash some of the living water onto my face. In an instant, I was hurtling back through time and space. I could see the planets whizzing by again. I saw my angelic escort by my side once more. I could see the earth below, and finally I saw the little house at 121 Beech Street.

In the instant that the living water touched my face, I was sucked back into my body and I arose from the shag carpet. It was now dark, and I was covered with sweat. I could still smell the fragrances of the Lord's garden, and the taste of the living water still lingered in my mouth. I could still hear the crescendo of angelic worship as it swirled around me at that moment.

When I looked at the clock, I was astonished to see that it was now well past 1 AM. I had been in my tiny prayer closet nearly ten hours. Or was I? I rose to my knees and found that it was still very difficult to move my body. When I got up to splash water on my face, I discovered gold specks there. I laughed and took a quick shower. Then I sat down at the keyboard of the old computer and started to write. As the sun began to rise, I lay down on my bed and fell asleep. Later I woke up dreaming about a lion licking my face and began to laugh again.

# CHAPTER 14

# PSALM 23
# SUFFER NOT THE LITTLE CHILDREN

*February 7, 2002, 10:46 PM*

This morning I experienced this passage of Scripture:

*Then they also brought infants to Him that He might touch them; but when the disciples saw it, they rebuked them. But Jesus called them to Him and said, "Let the little children come to Me, and do not forbid them; for of such is the kingdom of God. Assuredly, I say to you, whoever does not receive the kingdom of God as a little child will by no means enter it"* (Luke 18:15-17).

As I was praying in my little prayer closet, the Lord appeared to me in a vision. I saw Jesus again. He was beckoning me to come to Him. I saw the Lord with His hands outstretched. The Lord was waving at me, and He was motioning me to ascend into the heavens with Him. So I went! The instant that I purposed in my heart to go to the Lord, I was lifted up and felt as if I was leaving my body. I found my spirit soaring through a beautiful and colorful tunnel of light. This experience usually lasts for several minutes. When I landed, I found myself surrounded by angels. I know these four angels; I have seen them before.

The angels caught me as I landed, and then helped me to stand. It took a moment for me to get my balance, so the angels held me firmly but gently by my arms. As I looked at them, they smiled, which reassured me that everything was okay. I looked to my left and saw an angel that I know. His beautiful blue eyes sparkled with love and grace. He smiled at me and continued to hold me up.

I began to smell the wonderful fragrances of this place. Floral aromas and grasses abound here. I looked down at the stone pavers under my bare feet. They felt cool and smooth. I looked ahead and saw an ornate bed of manicured flowers that seemed to be worshiping Jesus. I could almost hear their beauty. I was filled with love and peace. I was so pleased to be in this place again. I glanced at the crystal blue sky and saw wispy clouds dancing by. I took another deep breath and inhaled Paradise again. The angel on my right let loose his grip and motioned to the meadow nearby.

When I looked in that direction, I saw the Lord. He was waiting for me in our usual spot. The angels had prepared a place for us. There was a small serving table and our beautiful quilts were laid side by side. Tenderly I broke free from my angelic friend's grip and ran to the Lord. I was again overcome with the power of His unconditional love and began to weep. Jesus smiled at me and welcomed me into His arms of love. I luxuriated in the arms of Christ and wept for a long time. Time seemed to stand still, and I could smell the fragrance of fresh-baked bread on His immaculate white robe. I inhaled again and relished the fragrance of God. Once again I was enveloped and overwhelmed by the glory of God.

Then the Lord spoke to me, "I love those who love Me, and those who seek Me early will find Me. True riches and honor are with Me, enduring riches and righteousness are found in Me. My fruit is better than gold, yes, than fine gold, and My revenue than choice silver. I traverse and walk the way of righteousness, and I move in the midst of the paths of justice. I will cause those who love Me to inherit wealth, and I will fill their treasuries with real riches."

Then the Lord peeled me away from His embrace and looked deeply into my eyes. Such beautiful eyes! Christ's eyes are so rich and loving. He held me at arm's length with both hands upon my shoulders and indicated that we should sit in the place that was prepared for us. What a wonderful time, and what a beautiful portrait of Christ, the Messiah, and the Savior of the world.

## FRESH-BAKED BREAD

When we sat down on the magnificent quilts, the sounds and perfume of Heaven invaded my senses in a fresh new way. I was lost in the wonder and the majesty of God's creation. The still crystal clear river meandered slowly by. No doubt it had an eternity to reach its destination. By the bank of the river, flowering trees swayed and worshiped God. They emitted a bouquet of heavenly fragrances. Flowers of innumerable variety also danced and swayed in the gentle breeze.

I looked at the small table between us. It was ornately and expertly crafted and inlaid with silver and gold patterns. It held a fresh-baked loaf of bread, fruit, and a crystal carafe of wine. Jesus took the loaf of bread and blessed it, giving the Father thanks for it this day. Then He broke a small piece off and handed it to me. When I took it from His right hand, I saw the nail scars, and tears began to form in my eyes. Jesus smiled again, and with His left hand put His index finger to his lips, signaling me to cease. So I wiped the tears from my eyes with the back of my right hand and took the bread from the Lord with my left hand.

An angel stepped up and poured red wine into a golden goblet that was intended for me. I tasted the bread and was amazed at the richness and goodness of its flavor. Setting my bread on the little serving table, I took the goblet and tasted the wine. It was rich and strong. It seemed that the flavor penetrated through every fiber of my being. At that instant, a short gust of wind blew my hair around, and I could hear the laughter of little children being carried upon the breeze. These children were singing and laughing with glee. I cocked my head to the side and listened to the melody for a moment. I noticed that Jesus was also listening and smiling with delight, too.

I looked down the meadow and saw the beautiful sunlight reflecting off the still waters as they meandered by. The light here created a cascade of rainbow colors in the air as the sun filtered through the shimmering cirrus clouds above. Butterflies flitted around the flowers and seemed to hover around the Lord. I watched them in amazement as they would from time to time land upon His shoulder for a moment. The butterflies gently touched Him with their colorful wings before taking flight again. It seemed to be an act of worship.

When I finished my bread and wine, I laid down on the quilt at the feet of Jesus. The Lord was sunning His bare feet in the warm air. I listened to His sayings for a long time, taking pleasure being in His presence and hearing His sweet voice. Christ's voice is like music to my ears; much like a symphony of excellent harps and soothing woodwinds, or the sounds of many soothing waters.

I was simultaneously enjoying the fragrances of the flowers and trees. Honeysuckle and jasmine lingered in the clear, clean air. Other delicate scents mingled with these, but I was not aware of what they were. They smelled wonderful to breathe in. The fragrances were alive, and it seemed that I could actually taste the fragrances of Heaven today.

I watched as one of the butterflies flew farther up into the green pasture. It was brilliant purple. For some reason I was drawn to this particular butterfly. After a while, I saw the group of small children I had heard singing earlier. One little girl began to chase the brilliant purple butterfly around and around. However, the butterfly flittered just out of the little one's reach, eluding her hands. Each time the little girl swooned and giggled as she reached out for the floating creature.

## HERE THEY COME!

I closed my eyes for a few minutes and luxuriated in Jesus' presence and in His sayings. After a time, the cheerful sound of laughter filled my ears again. The laughter was pure and full of joy. It filled my ears with delight and pleasure. I propped myself up on my right elbow to look for the source of the heavenly laugher. I saw dozens of little children running. They were in pursuit of the little girl with long, curly blond hair who was still seeking diligently to catch the brilliant purple butterfly. For the first time, I noticed that several angels were also running with these children. At that instant it occurred to me that these angels were the children's friends and caretakers. Jesus also sat up and looked around to His left saying, "Here they come! They are coming here!" This seemed to give the Lord great pleasure and satisfaction.

At that moment, the children jumped upon Jesus and they all tumbled over with a plop! Jesus laughed with the children and it seemed that He never wanted to stop. They played together in the grassy meadow. Jesus was full of laughter, smiles, and delight. The children formed a big circle and Jesus joined hands with two of them and they began to spin around and around. I realized that Jesus often plays with the children in this way. I jumped up and joined the children and their angels in the dance, and soon I was laughing and filled with delight too. Occasionally we would all tumble down together, and Jesus would wrestle with the children on the grass, laughing all the while.

After a time, I stepped away from the group and lay back down on my quilt. I was enjoying watching Jesus as He laughed and played with the children. It seems that He never wants to stop. Around and around they went. Oh, how Jesus loves the children. The angels also stood by and watched as God played with these little ones. "Suffer not the little ones when they come my way. For I love the little children, and now it is My turn to play," I heard Jesus say.

A few of the children stood by and watched with the angels and me. At that moment I noticed that the beautiful little girl with long, curly blond hair was still trying to catch the brilliant purple butterfly. As I watched, the purple butterfly floated on the gentle breeze and flew very close to me. As it passed by, I saw the sunlight reflect beautiful colors from its colorful purple wings. I suddenly understood why this little girl was seeking this butterfly so diligently. It was magnificent! In my heart I had a thought, or perhaps I may have uttered a little prayer. "Lord, I wish that I could give her that butterfly."

I watched in amazement as the brilliant purple butterfly circled around me twice. Each time it came a little closer. I held out my left hand and the butterfly landed upon my index finger. As it sat there opening and closing its wings for me, I could clearly see its intricacy and beauty, and I understood why the little blond girl had been chasing after it. When the butterfly landed upon my finger, the angels nearby swooned. This surprised me, and I looked up at the angels. Then I saw the curly blond-haired girl in a beautiful white dress running toward me. Her stunning blue eyes were big, and her face held a look of astonishment. When she stopped and stood close by, I could see her red freckles framing a big, beaming smile.

Slowly she reached out to my index finger and the beautiful purple butterfly that was sitting there. But at that moment, the butterfly took off again and fluttered away on the gentle wind. I also realized that all of the other children and Jesus had stopped playing and were watching this little heavenly drama unfold. I had a wish that the butterfly would return again. I watched in amazement as the butterfly circled to land upon my index finger a second time. A big smile creased the little girl's face and she stepped closer again. The butterfly was sunning itself on my index finger.

Slowly she raised her arm. Gently she placed the tip of her left index finger to the tip of my left index finger. Then the butterfly nimbly walked from my finger to hers. I knew that she really wanted to study the butterfly carefully, but it had always flown away from her grasp. They had played this game together for a long time. It was silent for an eternal moment. The little girl with the curly blond hair held the purple butterfly up into the sunshine just in front of her freckled face. She examined it for a minute or two and then held her hand up and said, "Goodbye." A gentle breeze carried the purple butterfly away riding the winds of Heaven once more.

## FLY FREELY

The angels were all looking on in amazement, as were Jesus and the other children. I did not quite understand. One of the angels spoke up saying, "She has been chasing that one special butterfly for eternity, and it has been given to her by your hand!" The angel that spoke seemed to be astonished. The little girl just let it fly away freely and began to chase it again, running back down the meadow with renewed enthusiasm. Soon all the other children and angels chased after her, singing and tumbling as they went.

Suffer not the little children, for this is truly their land. The angels in Heaven and children are singing. They are playing across the land—just as Jesus is playing and we can listen to His sayings. Jesus calls the little children to Him and sits in the midst of them and says:

> *Assuredly, I say to you, unless you are converted and become as little children, you will by no means enter the kingdom of heaven. Therefore whoever humbles himself as this little child is the greatest in the kingdom of heaven. Whoever receives one little child like this in My name receives Me* (Matthew 18:3-5).

Several years later as I read this document that I captured from that old computer, it struck me as powerful and possibly a parabolic experience. I committed a season of prayer to this vision. I believe what I saw and experienced in Heaven was real. Jesus does in fact love the children. The Lord especially loves those who are orphans. Perhaps many of the children I saw in Heaven in this experience had died prematurely of natural causes or accidents. However, it is also possible that most of the children I played with in Psalm 23 were aborted on earth. Nonetheless, God has a plan and a special place and home for all children in the heavenly realms. Please take a few moments to think about that now.

In the next chapter, we travel into the Father's vineyard to see how Jesus and God's angels are working in that amazing heavenly place.

# Chapter 15

# The Father's Vineyard

Jesus and I seemed to mount up as if on eagle's wings. In the next instant, I was soaring into the heights of the heavens. I saw the mountains far below, and in the far distance I could see the crystal cathedral of God. Emanating from the throne were brilliant lights and the sounds of worship such as I have never experienced. The crystal cathedral is also the source of the river of life. I saw it flow freely from the Father's throne, through the heavens, finally feeding the rivers that led into the great and massive vineyard. From this great height, the Lord allowed me to see the true vine.

The Lord took me up into the heights of Heaven and showed me the vineyard from a great distance. Then He took me into the Father's vineyard on sequential visits to the heavenly realms. Jesus led me as we explored the vast vineyard on these excursions. These trips into the vineyard took place over several weeks—we took many trips into the valley of the vineyard. We invested many days moving across the vast and massive plateau. The Father's vineyard covers hundreds of square miles. It is immense. The river of life flows and meanders through the middle of the ground and the center of the fields there. The plots of land in the vineyard are too numerous to number. It was from a great height that Jesus showed me the base of the great vine. The true vine is immense, and its circumference must be larger than the New Orleans Superdome, which by the way, is the home of the Saints. The beginning of the true vine must be at least ten times the size of a superdome. It is unimaginably large, and I have a difficult time describing its size. What an awesome God.

I had the revelation that even though the Father's vineyard is hundreds and hundreds of square miles, each individual vine is a branch of the one true vine. Over the course of several weeks, the Lord taught me in great detail that it is all one living vine. It is all one church. The vineyard is all His church and His bride. It was only after Jesus was absolutely certain that I completely understood this fact that He actually took me to the vineyard.

## ONE TRUE VINE

The first time I actually stepped into the vineyard, I was astounded at the enormity of it all. The Lord Jesus guided me into this incredible, massive, living entity. We were always accompanied by four angelic beings. There were also many angels who worked in the Father's vineyard. As we walked mile after mile, the Lord took the time to stop and point out different places and aspects of the true vine to me. Each time He asked me what I saw. Each time I would relate to the Lord what I saw. I told the Lord about the things I saw in as much detail as I could. Jesus was training me. I am certain that the lessons that Jesus taught the disciples as recorded in John 15 were in much greater detail than what is actually recorded in that gospel. Of course, this is only my opinion. It was apparent that Jesus knows every square inch of the vineyard and the true vine intimately.

That is exactly what the Holy Spirit is calling His church to today, a place of intimacy and communion with Jesus. It makes total sense that Jesus would seek a very close and personal relationship with His church and His people before His return. Jesus is calling the church to a place of friendship and intimacy. Jesus wants to know His bride personally!

We should find this very comforting. The Lord desires to have a very personal and intimate relationship with you as an individual, too.

As we walked mile by mile, the Lord pointed out certain branches of the true vine. One branch the Lord showed me was very clean and orderly. This part of the vineyard even had a nice white picket fence around its boundaries. It was a very large section of the vine and the grounds around it were very well-manicured and maintained. There were no weeds or tares in the rich soil near the vine. The ground had been tilled and manicured. This branch of the vineyard had many beautiful leaves upon it and they seemed to be quite healthy and in abundance.

I assumed that Jesus was very pleased with this vine. It looked very good, and it appeared to be very healthy. Then Jesus instructed me to take a closer look. I still liked the way this branch of the vine looked, and it seemed to be very healthy and vigorous. I was surprised when Jesus said, "This branch is due to be pruned by My Father soon." When the Lord said this, I noticed a group of angels nearby. They were working on the vine, pruning branches and bundling the woody materials in sheaves of sorts. I did not understand this statement because the branch looked so healthy (see John 15:1-2).

## FRUITFUL

Then I saw the Lord as He used His hand to reveal that though it had many leaves, this branch did not have very much fruit. The grapes were small and some were deformed. They had not developed correctly, and this was very unusual in the Father's vineyard. Jesus had to search under many leaves to even find these small unhealthy grapes. This particular vine was planted by the great river of living waters. Its leaves turned toward the sun and it was well-groomed. In fact, it was very orderly. Yet, it did not bear good fruit. There were a few nice grapes on this section of the true vine. There were some very nice grapes even, and some choice grapes. However, it seemed that most were not fit for harvest. Somehow I understood that the Lord only allowed grapes without spot or blemish to be harvested from the Father's vineyard. This also surprised me a little, but at the same time this fact also makes perfect sense in the Kingdom of Heaven (see Eph. 1:4; 5:25-27).

Over time, the Lord took great care to show me many branches of the true vine. Some looked very undone. They had weeds and tares in the ground around the base of the vine. The fence and trellis around some of these were broken down and in disrepair. This surprised me as well. The leaves upon these branches were not very attractive or pretty to look upon. Then the Lord took His right hand and, carefully moving a set of these imperfect leaves, He showed me a very large cluster of grapes from this section of the vine. What fruit! This cluster of grapes were large, juicy looking, and very beautiful. They seemed to glow in the evening sunshine, and I could see the reflection of Jesus on the skin of these grapes.

This branch of the vine had much more fruit upon it than I would have imagined. I expected this smaller and anemic-looking vine to not produce as much as the perfectly healthy and immaculate-looking section of the vine. But the fruit this vine was bearing was nothing short of a miracle. I thought, *This is the anointing and grace of the Holy Spirit at work.* When this thought crossed into my mind, the Lord smiled at me and nodded in agreement.

Jesus rose up from His knees and we continued to walk through the Father's vineyard for hours and hours. In fact, over the next several months I was allowed to return to the heavenly realms to visit the Lord Jesus many times. On each of these successive days we returned to the Father's vineyard. After the third day of visiting the true vine, it occurred to me that Jesus was showing me something very important. When this thought came into my mind, the Lord said to me, "It is important that you write down the things that you see here in this place." That is the reason I have recorded these observations from these walks throughout the Father's vineyard.

## MANY BRANCHES

During this season, the Lord showed me many branches, and we stopped to look at these in great detail. Often we invested a lot of time with individual sections of the true vine, and the Lord seemed to inspect every minute detail. Some of the branches were in great disrepair and in poor condition. However, that did not hinder the Lord from tenderly and lovingly caring for each one. At times I heard the Lord actually pray over a section of the true vine. Several times I noticed that angels came and cared for those areas of the vines immediately after Jesus moved on. Perhaps that is why some of the branches that were in bad condition remained fruitful. In fact, some of the shabbiest sections of the vine bore much fruit. Some vines in an unattended-looking condition had little or no fruit, but others in a similar condition had an unbelievable bounty of fruit.

Other sections of the vine that appeared to have greater care given to the soil and appeared to be well-tended seemed to have all leaves and very little or no fruit. Even some of the larger and healthier branches that grew very close to the river of life and seemed to be well-maintained had little or no fruit. This was a great surprise to me. In fact, I saw only a few of the large, healthy-looking branches growing near the water of life that actually had an abundance of fruit. I was amazed that some of the vines that were much farther from the source of water and seemed to have very small branches and few leaves had great amounts of fruit. As time progressed, I became certain that the Father's vineyard was a parabolic image of the Body of Christ and the church upon the earth.

One section of the true vine in particular stood out to me as Jesus and I inspected it. It was a very puny-looking branch. And this section of the vine was a great distance from the river of life. All of the branches around it were in a very poor condition. In fact, it appeared to me that some of those branches of the vine were about to die. This also surprised me. These branches had just a little withered fruit still remaining on them. But not the branch that Jesus was showing me. This particular branch did not have a great deal of fruit because it was very small. However, the grapes it was bearing were among some of the biggest and most beautiful grapes that Jesus had shown me in our extensive tour of the Father's vineyard.

When Jesus Himself pointed out this branch of the vine to me, I was very surprised. I noticed that there was a small spring of water nearby. Perhaps this pool was similar to an artesian well on earth. It was bubbling up from the dry ground near the base of this amazing branch of the true vine. Somehow I understood that this phenomenon, where water bubbled up into the midst of a dry and thirsty land, was very scriptural. And I made a mental note to search my old King James Bible when I returned home after this trip. Later I found this Scripture passage in the book of Isaiah with the help of the Holy Spirit:

> *Then the eyes of the blind shall be opened, and the ears of the deaf shall be unstopped. Then the lame shall leap like a deer, and the tongue of the dumb sing. For waters shall burst forth in the wilderness, and streams in the desert. The parched ground shall become a pool, and the thirsty land springs of water; in the habitation of jackals, where each lay, there shall be grass with reeds and rushes* (Isaiah 35:5-7).

At this point I became aware of the fact that as Jesus had been giving me a tour of the Father's vineyard over the past weeks, He was certainly seeking to teach me important lessons. And when I discovered those Scriptures from Isaiah 35, I was certain that they perfectly represented and confirmed what I had seen with Jesus earlier in the day. These Scriptures also gave me great hope because I was living in a very dry and parched place.

## CONNECTED TO THE ONE TRUE VINE

As I prayed about this, I became aware of the fact that the Lord was showing me things in a parabolic way. Of course, Jesus often taught and spoke in parables while He walked upon the earth. And when I realized this fact, it made perfect sense to me that the Lord would continue to use parabolic illustrations in the heavenly places. This fact gave me great peace and confirmation of the things I was experiencing in the heavenly realms. Though at times, the Lord spoke very clearly to me, as a man does to a friend, during our times together in the heavenly places.

As I continued to ascend into heavenly places during this extended season, the Lord Jesus continued to walk with me through the Father's vineyard. He continued to show me many different branches. We looked at all different types of branches which were connected to the one true vine. However, it seemed to me that Jesus was most pleased with the vines that did not seem to be in a likely place to flourish.

Time after time when the Lord discovered beautiful fruit growing upon scrawny or unhealthy sections of the one true vine, Jesus would break out into a broad smile. And I could actually feel the pleasure that the Lord took from these unlikely places. The Lord was well-pleased with the branches that had only a cluster or two of fruit. In fact, it seemed that He took great pleasure from sections of the vine like these more so than from the other larger and healthier looking branches, which had mostly leaves.

When we left the branch with the artesian spring, Jesus asked me to follow Him again. I always love to follow Jesus in the heavenly realms because I know that He is about to reveal hidden secrets or mysteries to me. And this is always very rewarding. We walked together for quite a way. It seemed to me that Jesus was very focused as we were walking through that part of the Father's vineyard. I continued to study the branches and the amount of fruit on each one as the Lord Jesus had taught me to do. It was amazing because of all of the different types of branches that were to be found in this remarkable part of Heaven. We were walking steadily up an incline in a section of the Father's vineyard that was cultivated upon higher elevations.

As we walked up a small grade, I noticed that there was a large cave in the hillside there. It was unusual and appeared to be the entrance to an old gold mine. It looked like something from the 1800s. I stopped and then walked over to look into the shaft. It was very difficult to see inside the mine. Jesus called out to me and told me to catch up to Him. I fell into step beside Jesus, and I asked Him about the old mine. The Lord told me not to be concerned about that particular place at this time. He seemed to be totally focused on a specific mission. We continued to walk purposefully, and after a while we came to a very small branch of the true vine. Jesus immediately knelt down beside it and began to inspect it very closely.

The main branch was very small and gnarled. It appeared to be very old. There were not very many leaves upon this small branch. However, the soil around the base of the vine was tilled and well-kept. There were just a few tares in this small spick-and-span part of the vineyard. This small vine had just a few clusters of grapes, but they were all very nice. The grapes on this vine were not the best, but they were very good looking grapes.

## VERY SPECIAL GRAPES

Jesus pulled back the leaves to show me a small cluster of three perfectly formed grapes. They were golden in color and there seemed to be an anointing of the Holy Spirit that emanated from the largest grape. I could tell that Jesus was personally very familiar with this grape. I was amazed that the Lord knew this one individual grape so well. There were millions and millions of grapes in the Father's vineyard. Yet, Jesus had walked miles to inspect this single grape on this day. It was as if He was being drawn to this particular grape. What Jesus did next surprised me.

He reached out with His right hand and plucked this very special grape from the one true vine. As Jesus held it in the palm of His hand, He looked intently at it. He told me to look at the grape too, and when I did, I went into a vision. I saw a little, grey-haired widow in her humble kitchen. She was kneeling beside her table with her elbows on the little wooden chair there. She was in prayer, and she was speaking directly to Jesus. I was surprised that I could hear her prayers as I knelt beside Jesus. She was blessing her morsel of lunch.

The Lord told me to listen carefully to her as she prayed. This was the first time He had ever done this. I was amazed that I could hear her perfectly as she prayed. The Lord was allowing me to hear what He could hear. Immediately I could feel the emotions and the heartache that she was experiencing. I understood the urgency and the spirit of her prayer. It was very pure. Her prayer was very humble. Somehow I knew everything about her as she prayed to Jesus. Perhaps as I knelt so close to Jesus He allowed me to have His revelation concerning this woman's prayers and needs.

Her name was Frances, but her friends and late husband, Earl, had called her Fannie May before they died. She was weeping as she prayed. I was overcome with her heartfelt prayer and gut-wrenching emotions she was experiencing at that instant. Her prayer touched my spirit deeply, and an unknown compassion welled up from someplace deep within me.

She was praying for her only son. Fannie May had not heard from him for years. She felt that she too was approaching the end of her days. Fannie called out in the name of Jesus. Perhaps that is what had drawn the Lord to this place today? She prayed, "Oh Jesus, I do not know where Timmy is. I do not know what he is about, but You do, Jesus. Oh God, please forgive me if I have done something to hurt him. If I have pushed Timmy away, oh Lord, I repent." I knew that she had been praying this prayer for a long time, and she had touched Jesus with her heartfelt words. She had brought the Lord close to her with the purity of her heart and her repentance as she earnestly called out to God today.

As this vision continued, the Lord looked at me and asked me what I would do? At this point, as the Lord held the grape in the palm of His right hand, we were catapulted through time and space. Jesus and I were instantly in the little kitchen with Fannie as she was on her knees in prayer. The four angels that usually accompany me and the Lord were also standing around the little table. I believe that at that moment Jesus actually appeared to her for a minute. Perhaps she saw the Lord's angels, too. She was overcome, and it seemed that she was filled with the Holy Spirit because she began to pray loudly and more intently.

## WHAT WOULD YOU DO?

Once again the Lord repeated His question to me, "What would you do?" Without thinking I instantly said, "Lord, touch the heart of her son so that he would call his mother after all these years." Instantly I was again traveling through time and space and found myself at a construction site. I recognized Timmy immediately because he had the gentle blue eyes of his mother. He was a carpenter, and he was working very hard. Jesus stepped up beside Timmy and spoke to him. He stopped hammering and put down his sixteen pound framing hammer, looking around for a moment. Jesus said, "Call your mother. Tell her that you love her. Tell her that you are going to come home to see her." It appeared that the Spirit of the Lord fell upon the young man, and he began to weep as something deep down within him had been broken instantly in that moment.

He left work immediately to find a phone. Suddenly we were back in the kitchen with Fannie May. She was still praying when the phone rang. She got up quickly from her knees and answered it. She knew in her spirit before she picked up the phone that it was her son who was calling. Her son repented and they spoke for a long time and started the process of healing their relationship. Timmy told Fannie May that he was going to come home. In fact, he told her that he would be there the next day. Tears of joy were streaming from her eyes and she turned and seemed to look at Jesus one last time. Fannie May smiled at the Lord and He smiled back at her.

## RECONNECTING TO THE ONE TRUE VINE

Instantaneously Jesus and I were back in the Father's vineyard. The Lord was still holding the perfectly formed grape in the palm of His right hand. I looked into the eyes of the Lord and saw that tears were trickling from His eyes. Then Jesus did something amazing. He took the grape and reattached it to the one true vine. This seemed to give

Him great pleasure and a smile beamed across His face, and His tears stopped. It was then that I also realized that I was crying, too.

The Lord and I stood up and began to walk back through the Father's vineyard together. Neither of us spoke for a long while. However, I was astonished at what I had just witnessed. For the first time I noticed that the anointing of the Holy Spirit seemed to be emanating from many of the other grapes that grew upon the various vines that we passed. I pondered why Jesus was drawn to the place and vine that we had visited today.

Jesus turned and smiled at me valiantly and then said, "For I know the thoughts that I think toward you, thoughts of peace and not of evil, I desire to give you a future and a hope. When you will call upon Me, and go and pray to Me, I will listen to you. And when my people seek Me they will surely find Me. You search for Me with all your heart and I will be found by you" (see Jer. 29:11-14). I remembered that Jesus had spoken those very same words over me during the first visitation of Jesus I had experienced in Springdale, Newfoundland, Canada, on November 25, 2001.

As I looked into the eyes of Jesus, revelation began to flow into my spirit about God's heart to answer all of our prayers. The Lord knows what we have need of before we even ask, but sometimes when we search for Him, He waits until the perfect time to respond. Today was the perfect time for Jesus to answer Fannie May's prayer. It was a great privilege and honor to witness such a supernatural event! In fact, it was astonishing to see a prayer answered. God is listening and He will answer your prayers, too.

# HEAVEN AND YOU

Heaven—is it real?

Is Heaven actually a real place that we can expect to visit, or perhaps spend eternity?

The truth is that there is a benevolent, kind, and all-loving God who created each of us in His image. As such, the Lord has gone before us to prepare a place or abode for you and me to exist and live abundantly in His presence throughout all of eternity. Our spirits will certainly live on forever. God has created us in His very image. As such, we are eternal beings.

God has such an intense and intimate love for you that He sent His only begotten Son, so that you have a way to be reunited with Him infinitely in Heaven. I am a witness of this. Heaven *is* real. You have been given a wonderful choice and privilege to choose Heaven as your eternal home. The descriptions of the heavenly realms that I have shared in this short book are only mere glimpses into Paradise. We will spend our days in Heaven learning more about God and His Kingdom.

We will continue to grow and mature into the very image and stature of Jesus. For many people this will be the very desire of their hearts. We will grow and learn. We will invest our days exploring and discovering the hidden mysteries of Christ's Kingdom. We will have the privilege to explore the vastness of all of the realms of Heaven. We will travel to numerous heavenly places.

I imagine that each of us will experience Heaven differently. Some may invest eternity fishing in the river of life that flows through Psalm 23. Some will spend their time reading in the Father's massive library. Others may seek to worship the Lord in Spirit and in truth around the very throne of God. And others will pursue the very desires of their heart perfecting their giftings by creating music, literature, and masterpieces of art.

## YES, HEAVEN IS REAL

Let me share one final depiction of Heaven with you. On one occasion, I had been taken up into the heavenly realms to join Jesus in the great banquet hall. After we had concluded our meal and fellowship time together, the Lord arose from the table. He smiled at me and said, "I want you to come with me today. There is something important that I want to show you."

Jesus walked to the far eastern wall of the great banquet hall, and I walked in sync with Him. There was an excitement in my heart about what the Lord was going to reveal to me. By now I had been visiting the Lord for months in the heavenly realms. In my humanness, I had thought that I had "seen it all." How silly was that idea? The Lord led me to a wonderfully ornate door. It was baroque-looking and covered with ornate and lavish designs. It appeared to be covered in pure gold. The heavenly light that was filtering down from the windows above created an ethereal glow within the very material of the double doors. For a moment I wondered why I had not noticed these marvelous doors before. Then I remembered that the hidden mysteries of Heaven need to be revealed by God.

Two of the four angels that were walking with Jesus and me moved to open the doors as we approached. When the angels opened the doors, the sound of worship exploded into the great banquet hall. Jesus entered into a magnificent hallway that led upward at a slight angle. When I stepped into the hallway, my eyes were momentarily blinded by the glory and power of the brilliant light emanating from the other end of the corridor. Looking down at my bare feet, I saw that I was walking on a golden pathway and this helped magnify the luminous light that was flooding into this hidden passageway. I could feel the coolness of the material of the floor, and I could also feel the tangible glory of God flowing passed me in waves and billows. The heavy, weighty, tangible glory of God poured passed me like a mighty rushing wind in this place. It was wonderful, and I could have just camped out there.

Tears began to leak from my eyes as the weighty glory of God filled my spirit. Jesus reached out with His right arm and put His hand on my shoulder, drawing me closer to Himself; we continued to walk together. As we reached the end of the very long corridor, the Lord stopped and turned to look deeply into my eyes. The fragrances of frankincense and myrrh that I had been experiencing over the past few months were powerful and permeated the air that was rushing over us from the room that was just a few yards ahead. As Jesus gazed into my eyes, the brilliant glory from the room twinkled and shimmered from His beautiful irises. Jesus smiled at me with delight. He said, "You are always welcome in this place. Come with Me now." My heart leapt with joy at these words, and I wondered where the Lord was taking me today.

With that, He turned and purposely moved forward, stepping through a portal into the room. I was immediately awed by the volume of the sounds in this place. I looked out to see millions and millions of people worshiping God. The sounds of worship permeated the air, and it was obvious that thousands of angels were singing in unison with the millions of people I saw. In fact, there were millions of angels in this place, too. I was reminded of how I had first heard angelic singers in Newfoundland back in 2001. (This incident is depicted in *Dancing with Angels 1.)* This thought made me smile. I was actually flabbergasted by the sight that lay before me. Jesus continued to walk deliberately toward the center of this massive room. On either side of us were people dressed in immaculate white robes. The Lord and I were walking down a wide row that appeared to be fashioned of a golden crystalline substance. The four angels who always accompanied me in the heavenly realms were walking in step with us as we approached the center of the room.

Most of the saints in the room were so involved and engrossed in worship that they did not notice Jesus as He walked by. Occasionally, people would see the Lord and would fall on their faces and worship the Lamb of God as He passed by. The people and angelic hosts were singing incredibly beautiful and harmonious praises to God. The sound was the most beautiful sound that I have ever heard. They were worshiping the Lamb of God and singing songs of glory and honor to Jesus. There was such a powerful presence of unity, peace, and all-consuming love in this enormous place that it was simply overwhelming. I was totally enamored by what I was seeing, feeling, hearing, and experiencing.

We walked into the room from the very outer edge. I was astonished; and in my mind I tried to calculate the number of individuals who were in this glorious place. It dawned on me how the apostle John must have felt when he wrote:

> *I looked, and I heard the voice of many angels around the throne, the living creatures, and the elders; and the number of them was ten thousand times ten thousand, and thousands of thousands, saying with a loud voice: "Worthy is the Lamb who was slain to receive power and riches and wisdom, and strength and honor and glory and blessing!"* (Revelation 5:11-12).

# THE THRONE OF GOD

The Lord continued to move steadily through the massive group of people. From the top of the path that we were on, I began to understand that we were in an enormous room full of glory and ethereal light. Looking to the center I saw the source of the light. It was the throne of God. It appeared to be about a mile or more away from us now. However, I could see incredible lights phosphorescing within and around the throne. The Father's throne appeared to be covered in dense luminescent clouds, and every so often lightning and thunder would rumble forth from the midst of the glory making me wince. After a few claps of thunder and several flashes of lightning, I became more comfortable with the mighty noises and flashing lights that were being emitted from the area of the throne. This spectacle was still quite unnerving. I was quite undone to be in this place, and the reverential fear of the Lord fell upon me. Had I not been in the company of Jesus, I would have possibly collapsed.

It became obvious to me that Jesus was headed to the throne. This understanding gave me pause. The closer we got to the throne, the greater the reverential fear of the Lord grew within my spirit. As we proceeded toward the throne, I purposed in my heart to study my surroundings carefully. It is actually impossible for me to accurately depict the vastness and scale of the room that the Lord and I were walking through at that moment. It is possible that the throne room was miles in circumference. However, I am certain that the room was somewhat circular with the Father's throne located perfectly in the center.

There was a crystal cathedral-type ceiling soaring high above the room. Around the throne was a lake or sea of crystal that flowed from and around the throne. Both of these continuously reflected the lightning and glory that emanated from the Father's throne. As Jesus and I continued to walk down the sloping walkway leading to the center of the room, I continued to examine my surroundings. There were millions upon millions of people clad in white attire in this place worshiping God with vigor that I have never witnessed upon the earth. The experience of being in the throne room changed my life.

Once I turned to see Jesus smiling at me as I was looking around—taking in my surroundings. My investigation seemed to cause a bright smile to fill the Lord's face, and He placed His hand on my back again. After some time, we began to draw closer to the throne. The sound of the worship was so loud and intense that the very ground under my feet seemed to quake. It was then that I began to notice angelic beings that were flying around the throne. The colors and the glory that emanated from the throne made it difficult to look at it for longer than a second. However, it appeared to me that these angels were moving acrobatically in and through the glory surrounding the throne. They were singing and worshipping loudly and with a supernatural passion. As these angels darted about, their multifaceted wings dispersed the glory of God in all directions at once. Phosphorescent colors cascaded in all directions around the throne to be reflected by the crystal cathedral and the waters surrounding the throne.

As we drew nearer, I saw that the Father's throne was surrounded by other smaller very luxuriant chairs constructed of gold and red velvet. Each chair was of Victorian-looking design and had very ornate carvings on the arms and legs. These chairs were quite large and had similar styled footstools at each one. It dawned on me that these were for the twenty-four elders. Although when I sought to look at them, I was unable to see them clearly as they were bathed in light and glory.

Jesus continued to walk toward the throne. When we reached the bottom of the platform, I saw twelve large stairs leading up to the throne area. These large stairs seemed to be made of gemstones like diamonds, rubies, sapphires, mother of pearl, topaz, emerald, turquoise, amethyst, and others perhaps, but I am not sure. They emanated the glory and lights around the throne in a brilliant reflection. Each step was about eighteen inches in height.

For a moment, the words "mercy and justice" flashed upon these foundational steps of the throne. When Jesus began to walk up the steps, I noticed that there was a magnificent place established for Him on the right hand of the Father. Remaining at the bottom of the throne, I stood still like a statue, paralyzed by the reverential fear of God and the intense glory. Thunder once more roared in my ears and lightning bolted over my head at that instant illuminating the ceiling and the crystalline waters as Jesus sat down upon His throne. I closed my eyes and fell on my face and remained in that position for a long time. I entered into the worship of the Lord with all of my spirit and soul—the sensation was exhilarating and amazing.

## THE TANGIBLE FEAR OF THE LORD

After a long time, a persistent buzzing sound filled my ears, and I looked up to see a large angelic being hovering near my head. It was similar to the angels that I had seen in the vault of mantles. Slowly I rose up on my knees to see the cherubim dart back into the phosphorescent glory of the Father that was radiating around and from within the throne. In this place the tangible fear of the Lord was overwhelming, and for a moment I wondered if I was going to live.

At that instant, I looked up to see Jesus sitting at His rightful place at the right hand of the Father. The Lord smiled at me, and once again hope bubbled up within my spirit that I might live and not die. Jesus motioned me to join Him. Astonished, I stood up on my wobbly legs and walked slowly up the twelve stairs to stand on the right side of Jesus (see Rev. 3:21). My senses were overloaded by the sights and sounds surrounding the throne. The power of God's glory in this place is impossible for me to describe accurately. The volume of the sounds and the sheer size of this crystal cathedral of God were too much for my human mind to comprehend in that moment.

It took a long time, but gradually I began to adjust to the overwhelming and tangible presence of the glory that was radiating from this place. Jesus made a gesture to me with His chin indicating that I should turn around and look out into the massive room. I had been watching and observing Jesus for a long time. I was totally absorbed in the majesty and grandeur of the Messiah as He sat upon the throne. Truly, Jesus is the High Priest forever according to the order of Melchizedek (see Ps. 110:4, Heb. 6:20). I did not want to leave His presence nor did I wish to look at anything else in this place save for my Savior. There was no need to pray or even think. I just wanted to luxuriate in being here in the very presence of the Most High God.

At that moment I realized that tears were flowing from my eyes, and my heart was burning with a love and passion for God that I had never known. I looked into the eyes of Jesus again. Once more the Lord smiled at me and He raised His chin slightly for a second time indicating that I should look around. I turned around to look upon the masses of people gathered around the throne. Below the river of God reflected the glory of the throne in unison and in harmony with the vaulted crystal ceilings of this amazing and magnificent room. These created perfect acoustics for the worship that was ongoing in this massive crystal cathedral. Millions and millions of saints in white robes were arranged in a massive circle around the Father's throne. Angels of various kinds were worshiping the Lord in unison with these saints. There were balconies at various levels where angels sang and played musical instruments worshiping God in spirit and in truth in unison with the millions of saints below.

The throne room was perhaps miles in circumference. At one point I heard a massive clap of thunder and I realized that something was about to transpire. Perhaps this was what the Lord had wanted me to witness. My attention was drawn to the area in front of the center of the platform, which surrounds the throne. I saw a young man approach the throne of the Lord, and he was accompanied by several angels. His head was bowed, and he was trembling in great fear. Somehow I knew that it was time for this man to stand before God. I saw two large books brought to the Father's throne by angelic beings. I understood that these books were this person's books of life. The books in the angel's hands were similar to the millions of books that I had seen in the Father's library earlier.

## JUDGMENT DAY

One of the elders came forward and began to read from one of the books. This elder's stature was regal and his hair was so white that it seemed to glow. His words were clearly pronounced and articulated perfectly. The elder spoke for what seemed like hours sharing in great detail events from the man's life. As he spoke, images of the events were visible above the throne. All the while the glory of God emanated and shot out from around the throne. I heard a sound and saw Jesus rise up and walk down to stand beside the man. The Lord began to speak on the young man's behalf. I was not able to understand the words that Jesus was saying, but I understood that Jesus was offering a defense for this man. Jesus acted as an advocate just as a trial lawyer would defend someone in a court of law on earth.

This man had made Christ his Savior on earth and had not denied the Lord. And at this moment, Jesus was defending him before the Father and the elders around the throne. This man's sins had been washed clean by the blood of the Messiah. He was about to enter into Heaven for eternity as Christ spoke upon his behalf. Perhaps what I was seeing was what Jesus referred to as the resurrection of the just in Luke chapter 14. In that passage, the Lord referred to how people of the earth would receive a reward in Heaven for their genuine benevolent acts on earth.

As I watched this scene unfold before me, I understood that this man's gifts to the poor and alms were coming up before the Father (see Acts 10:4). I also understood that he was going to reap a heavenly reward for the things that he had done during his earthly life to help those who were less fortunate than him. I watched as this man received a beautiful crown of righteousness from one of the elders in attendance. At the command of Christ, two angels came forward to place a brilliant white robe upon the young man's shoulders. The young man then turned to join the millions who worshiped God in unison. I was amazed by what I was experiencing.

After a moment, the Lord returned to His place at the right hand of the Father. However, over the next several hours I watched this scenario play out time and time again. I may have actually been in this place for days, but later when I returned to my prayer room, I was surprised to find that only about nine hours had passed. I must have witnessed hundreds of individuals come to stand before the throne of the Father.

I watched as their lives were played out in the midst of the heavenly realms. For each one of those who knew Jesus as Savior and Messiah, I saw Jesus stand and contend on their behalf. Jesus defended them, and many were granted new robes, and some received crowns of righteousness (see 1 Timothy 4:8, James 1:12, 1 Pet. 5:4, Rev. 2:10). I understood that their sins were no longer recorded in their books of life, and they were given heavenly rewards and crowns of righteousness. I also saw many saints who received beautiful golden and jeweled crowns of life and righteousness and then lay their heavenly treasures at the feet of Jesus before the Father's throne (see Rev. 4:10).

Each time this transpired, the entire congregation of millions would begin to praise the Lord Jesus saying, "Worthy is the Lamb who was slain to receive power and riches and wisdom, and strength and honor and glory and blessing! Blessing and honor and glory and power be to Him who sits on the throne, and to the Lamb, forever and ever!" Then there was a thunderous chorus of "Amen!" and the whole family of God would worship the Lord once more. I witnessed this dramatic scene time and time again. I am certain that time as we know it was suspended or perhaps supernaturally expanded during this nine hour visitation to heaven.

After I had seen several people approach the throne to stand before the one true Holy and Righteous God, it occurred to me that these individuals' eternal destinies were being decided. The Lord was rewarding them based on the choices each had made and how they had lived their earthly lives. An intense desire to pray for each one welled up inside me, and I began to intercede for each one in turn. Some did not receive new robes or crowns of righteousness. It appeared that Jesus wept when this happened, and I would pray all the more. After a long time, I turned to see Jesus motion me, calling me to Himself.

## CONSIDER CAREFULLY

I walked over to look into the eyes of the Messiah, and understanding filled my heart of the magnitude of the sacrifice He had made for all humankind. I began to weep and mourn for those who were turned away. I saw that many were cast into what appeared to be outer darkness (see Matt. 8:12, 25:30). I held my face in my hands as if to hide my tears from the Lord, and then I felt His gentle, warm hands on my shoulders. I looked up to see Jesus looking deeply and passionately into my eyes. He said, "Consider carefully what you have seen and heard here today. Write down all things that you have seen and heard—and remember, you are always welcome here." I understood that every tongue, tribe, and nation are welcome to be in this place with God, too.

The Lord smiled and embraced me once more. As He wrapped His arms of love around me, I was filled with the sense of God's unconditional, unimaginable, and indescribable love for me once again. The sensation was similar the night of November 25, 2001 when the Lord Jesus stood over me in Newfoundland and I had been filled with understanding of the Messiah's unbelievable love for all humankind.

Jesus released me from His tender embrace and smiled at me one last time. Then Jesus descended the twelve steps once more to meet a new arrival at the foot of the Father's throne of mercy, judgment, and grace. I fell to my knees and began to pray for the young woman who stood at the foot of God's throne alone. She reminded me of my daughters. She appeared to quake with fear and trembling. When I rose, I was back in my prayer room, and tears were pooling on the old shag carpet below me. The fragrances of frankincense and myrrh lingered in the air, and I could still hear that angelic worship swirling around me. I remained on my knees weeping and interceding for various people for a long time. Later, I began to ponder these things in my heart and searched my old King James Bible for answers.

It has been more than a decade since this event occurred, and I have never shared it until now. In my heart, I have often thought of Ephesians chapter 2 when I have pondered this visit to the throne room over the years. That passage says:

> *Even when we were dead in trespasses, [God] made us alive together with Christ (by grace you have been saved), and raised us up together, and made us sit together in the heavenly places in Christ Jesus, that in the ages to come He might show the exceeding riches of His grace in His kindness toward us in Christ Jesus.*

*For by grace you have been saved through faith, and that not of yourselves; it is the gift of God, not of works, lest anyone should boast* (Ephesians 2:5-9).

Surely the salvation that God had given humankind comes from the finished work of the Messiah and Savior, Jesus Christ of Nazareth. And there is no other name by which men and women might be saved and restored to right relationship to God. Salvation is a gift of grace, no doubt. However, the Scriptures also tell us that everyone who will ever live upon the earth will stand before the throne of God. King Solomon stated this matter well in Ecclesiastes 12:13-14 saying:

*Let us hear the conclusion of the whole matter: Fear God and keep His commandments, for this is man's all. For God will bring every work into judgment, including every secret thing, whether good or evil.*

Jesus Himself spoke of the judgment day in Matthew 12:36-37 teaching us, *"But I say to you that for every idle word men may speak, they will give account of it in the day of judgment. For by your words you will be justified, and by your words you will be condemned."* In fact, Scripture is replete with examples of how we will all stand before God one day.

Perhaps in His mercy and grace the Lord allowed me to witness the throne and a tiny portion of the resurrection of the just. As I searched the Scriptures, I found that Revelation 20:11-12 depicts the best scriptural confirmation to the throne room encounter that I experienced:

*Then I saw a great white throne and Him who sat on it, from whose face the earth and the heaven fled away. And there was found no place for them. And I saw the dead, small and great, standing before God, and books were opened. And another book was opened, which is the Book of Life. And the dead were judged according to their works, by the things which were written in the books.*

I am certain of one thing: Heaven is real and God wants you to spend eternity there.

I remained in prayer for another full day considering everything I had seen and heard just as Jesus had instructed me. I searched the Scriptures seeking confirmation. I have often asked myself, *What will happen on the day I stand before my heavenly Father?* I have considered this question for many years, and I continue to ponder these things in my heart even today.

What about you? Have you considered these things? Are you 100 percent sure about where you will stand with God when you find yourself before the throne of the Father? Will Jesus stand at your side as your advocate and mighty counselor? (See Isaiah 9:6, 1 John 2:1.) If you are not certain where you stand before God, perhaps you may wish to pray the following prayer—because Heaven is real.

### Prayer of Salvation

The Word of God gives us simple steps to become a new creation and to enter into God's family.

You can inherit eternal life and live forevermore in Paradise, or Heaven.

If you believe in your heart that Jesus Christ of Nazareth is the Son of the living God and that He died upon the cross to pay for your sins, you can be saved.

Romans 10:10 tells you how to be born again, *"With the heart one believes unto righteousness, and with the mouth confession is made unto salvation."*

If you believe this, just pray this simple prayer:

*Dear heavenly Father, I confess Jesus Christ as Lord. I believe with my heart that Jesus is the Son of God and that He shed His blood and was crucified to pay for my sins. I believe that Jesus did rise from the dead on the third day. I believe that Jesus is alive, and that He will save me now. Lord, I am a sinner. I ask*

*You to forgive my sins and to save me right now. In Jesus' name I pray, Amen.*

*Lord, I thank You that I am saved! I am a new creature, and I am now in the family of God, I have become the righteousness of God!*

If you prayed that prayer, we want to hear from you. We want to send you a free gift from King of Glory Ministries International. Contact us with your address, and we will gladly send a free gift to congratulate you on your decision!

## ENDNOTE

1. Also see Ecclesiastes 12:14; Luke 9:26, 14:14; Acts, 10:42, 17:31; Romans 2:6,16, 14:10-12; 1 Corinthians 3:8; 2 Corinthians 5:10-11; Matthew 7:21-23, 16:27, 25:31, 26:64; Mark 8:38, John 5:22, 12:48; 2 Timothy 4:1; 1 Peter 4:5; Revelation 2:23, 20:12, 22:12.

# AUTHOR AND MINISTRY CONTACT INFORMATION

Kevin and Kathy would love to hear your testimonies about angelic encounters for possible use in future publications. To submit testimonies contact them by email.

King of Glory Ministries International is available to teach the material covered in this book in much greater depth in our *Dancing with Angels School of the Supernatural*. This school is available in DVD and CD sets. For more information or to order resources from Kevin Basconi, please visit our Web page at: www.kingofgloryministries.org.

**Email:** info@kingofgloryministries.org

Phone: 336-921-2825 or 816-308-2786

Mailing Address:

King of Glory Ministries International
PO Box 903
Moravian Falls, NC 28654

# Moravian Falls Miniature Art Gallery

When Kevin Basconi visited Jesus in Heaven the Lord spoke to him telling Kevin; "I have called you to be an artist, an author, and an evangelist". Kevin has sought to be obedient to the Lord in this. To see some of Kevin's art at the Moravian Falls Miniature Art Gallery, please visit our online art gallery to help support our ongoing humanitarian outreaches to build homes for at-risk children and feed widows and orphans at: www.MoravianFallsminiatureartgallery.com. A portion of the sales of all art purchased from this site will be used to help feed orphans in undeveloped nations. Thanks for your support in this worthwhile cause.

*Donate directly to our humanitarian works from Canada, the United States, or the United Kingdom.* You can also donate directly to our humanitarian work in undeveloped countries. If you are a citizen of Canada, the United States, or the United Kingdom, you can give directly through Hope For The Nations, and your gift will be tax deductible in your home country. Look for the Hope For The Nations link on the King of Glory Ministries Web page: www.hopeforthenations.com.

# King of Glory Ministries International

King of Glory Ministries International is all about the commission of Jesus Christ. The words of Isaiah 61 can be used to concisely summarize the call of our ministry:

> *The Spirit of the Lord GOD is upon Me, because the LORD has anointed Me to preach good tidings to the poor; He has sent Me to heal the brokenhearted, to proclaim liberty to the captives, and the opening of the prison to those who are bound; to proclaim the acceptable year of the LORD, and the day of vengeance of our God; to comfort all who mourn, to console those who mourn in Zion, to give them beauty for ashes, the oil of joy for mourning, the garment of praise for the spirit of heaviness; that they may be called trees of righteousness, the planting of the LORD, that He may be glorified* (Isaiah 61:1-3).

We, Kevin and Kathy Basconi, have sought to preach the Gospel of the Kingdom to the lost in many nations. As of this writing, we have visited more than thirty nations and five continents to proclaim the truth of Christ's total salvation and healing message—the Gospel of the Kingdom that Jesus instructed His disciples to proclaim. (See Matthew 4:23, 9:35, 24:14.) We have preached to hundreds of thousands of people and have seen tens of thousands make the decision to receive Jesus Christ as

Lord and Savior. We continue to minister in large crusade outreaches in Africa and other nations today as opportunity allows, and as the Spirit leads. We also minister in churches, King of Glory International Schools, and conference meetings in various nations.

The other critical calling of King of Glory Ministries International is to minister the love of the Father to widows and orphans. This humanitarian aspect of our call is defined in James 1:27 and Psalm 68:5. James 1:27 says, *"Pure and undefiled religion before God and the Father is this: to visit orphans and widows in their trouble, and to keep oneself unspotted from the world."* God has birthed in us a heart to minister in deed and not word alone. We also see this aspect of the Father's heart in Psalm 68:5, *"A father of the fatherless, a defender of widows, is God in His holy habitation."* (See the Orphanage tab on our Web page for more information about this important aspect of King of Glory Ministries International.)

## ABOUT KEVIN AND KATHY BASCONI

Kevin and Kathy Basconi are ordinary people who love an extraordinary God and co-founded King of Glory Ministries International. They have a heart to share the Gospel with the poor and the love of the Father to widows and orphans. They have visited thirty nations preaching the gospel and demonstrating the Kingdom of God in churches, conferences, and crusade meetings. They live in the mountains where they pursue a lifestyle of intimacy with Jesus.

Kevin is an ordained minister accredited with World Ministry Fellowship of Plano, Texas.

King of Glory Ministries International is also connected to the apostolic leadership of Pastor Alan and Carol Koch of Christ Triumphant Church located in Lee's Summit, Missouri.

9/6/20

# OTHER BOOKS BY KEVIN BASCONI

*Dancing with Angels 1—How to Work with the Angels in Your Life.*

*Dancing with Angels 2—The Role of the Holy Spirit and Open Heavens in Activating Angelic Encounters in Your Life*

*31 Word Decrees that Can Revolutionize Your Life*

*God's Prophetic Warning for America; Pray for the Peace of Jerusalem Now!*

*Coming soon: Angels and Orphans*

12/14/13     12/16/13   3/24/18

very different
Jesus has a library wa
He reads out He is all knowing p. 104
uses KJV
p. 148 Jesus had to rest
addicted to wine